Year 2
Textbook 2C

Series Editor: Tony Staneff

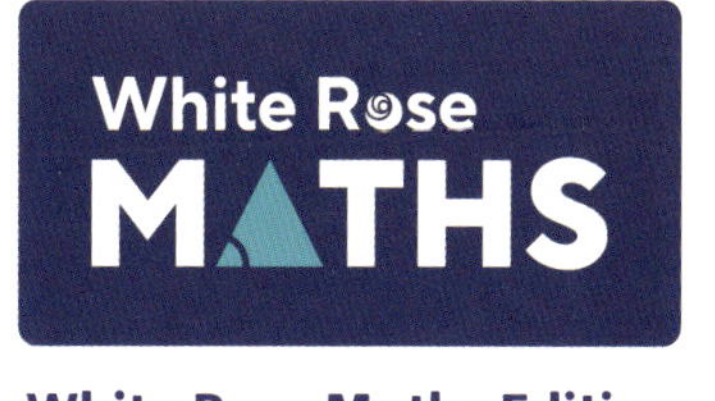

Flo

Flo is flexible.

She likes to help if you get stuck.

helpful

Sparks

brave

Astrid

curious

Ash

determined

Dexter

Series editor: Tony Staneff

Lead author: Josh Lury

Consultants (first edition): Professor Liu Jian and Professor Zhang Dan

Author team (first edition): Kelsey Brown, Jenny Lewis, Josh Lury, Stephen Monaghan, Beth Smith, Paul Wrangles, Liu Jian, Zhang Dan, Hou Huiying and Huang Lihua

Contents

Are you ready
for the next
part of our
maths journey?

How to use this book

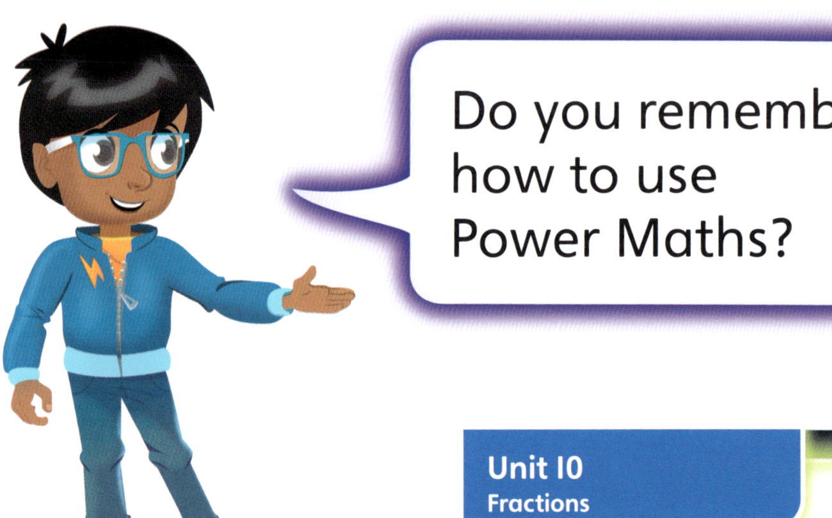

These pages help us get ready for a new unit.

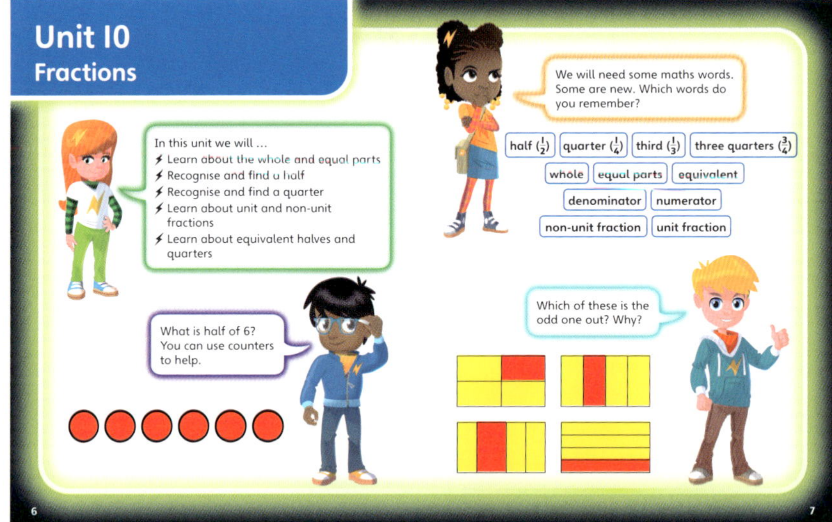

Discover

Lessons start with Discover.

Have fun exploring new maths problems.

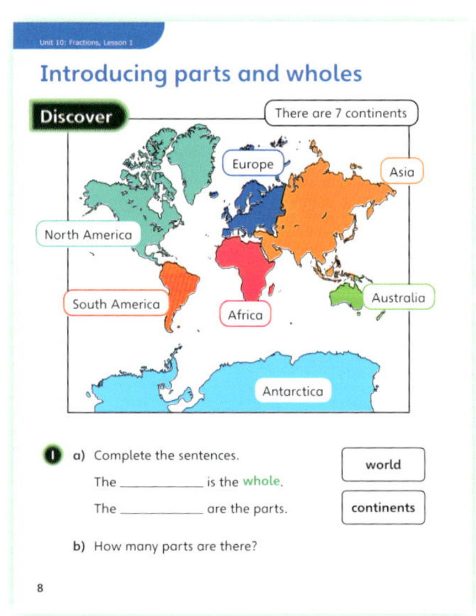

Share

Next, we share what we found out.

Did we all solve the problems the same way?

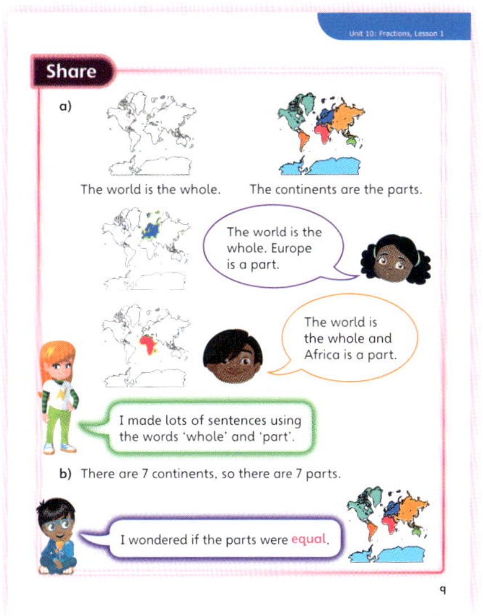

Think together

Then we have a go at some more problems together.

We will try a challenge too!

This tells you which page to go to in your Practice Book.

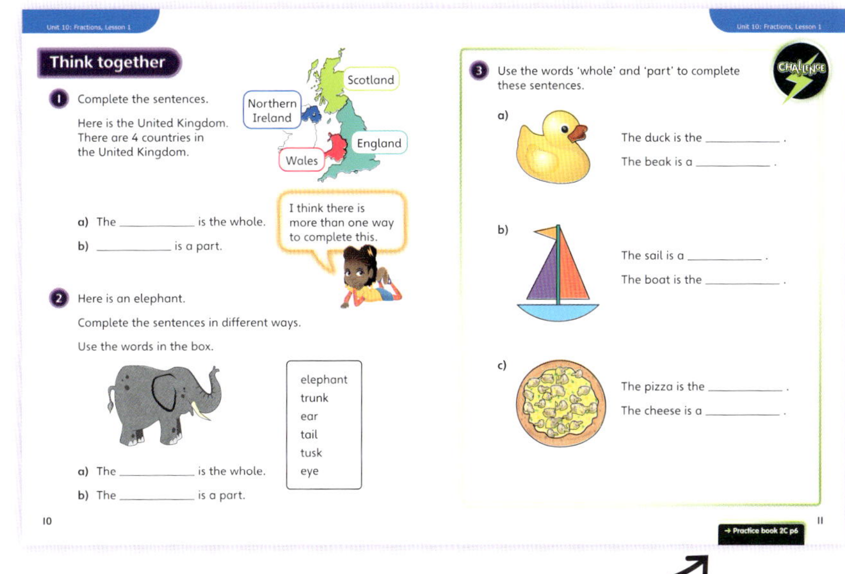

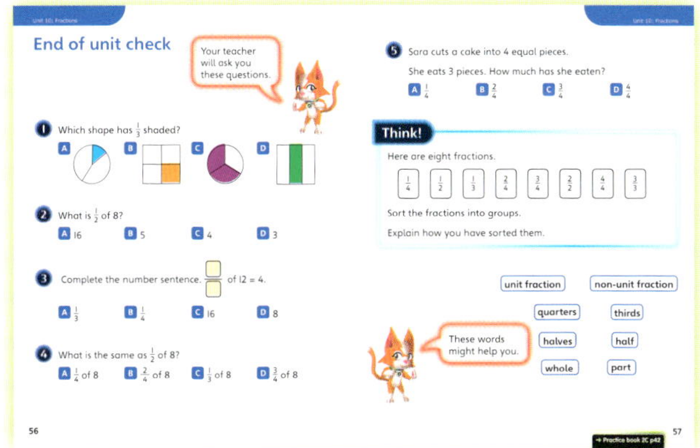

Unit 10
Fractions

In this unit we will …
- ⚡ Learn about the whole and equal parts
- ⚡ Recognise and find a half
- ⚡ Recognise and find a quarter
- ⚡ Learn about unit and non-unit fractions
- ⚡ Learn about equivalent halves and quarters

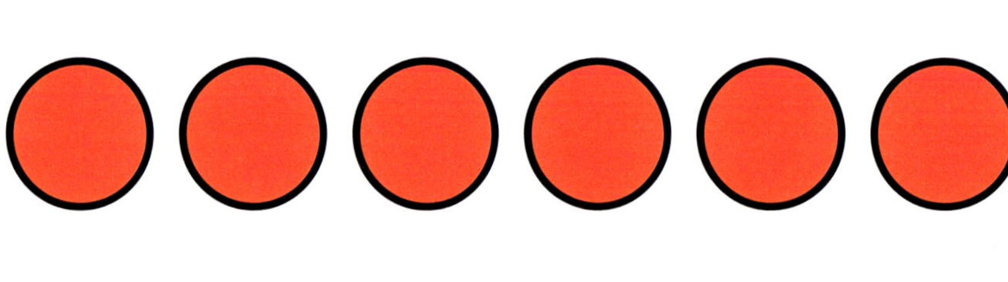

half ($\frac{1}{2}$) quarter ($\frac{1}{4}$) third ($\frac{1}{3}$) three quarters ($\frac{3}{4}$)

whole equal parts equivalent

denominator numerator

non-unit fraction unit fraction

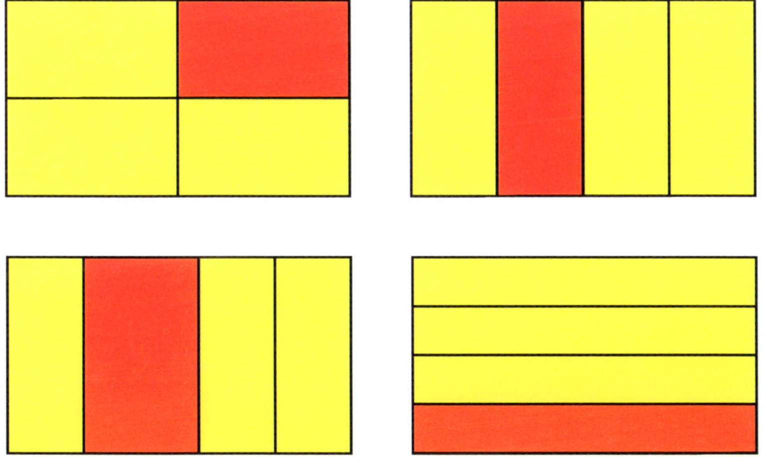

Introducing parts and wholes

Discover

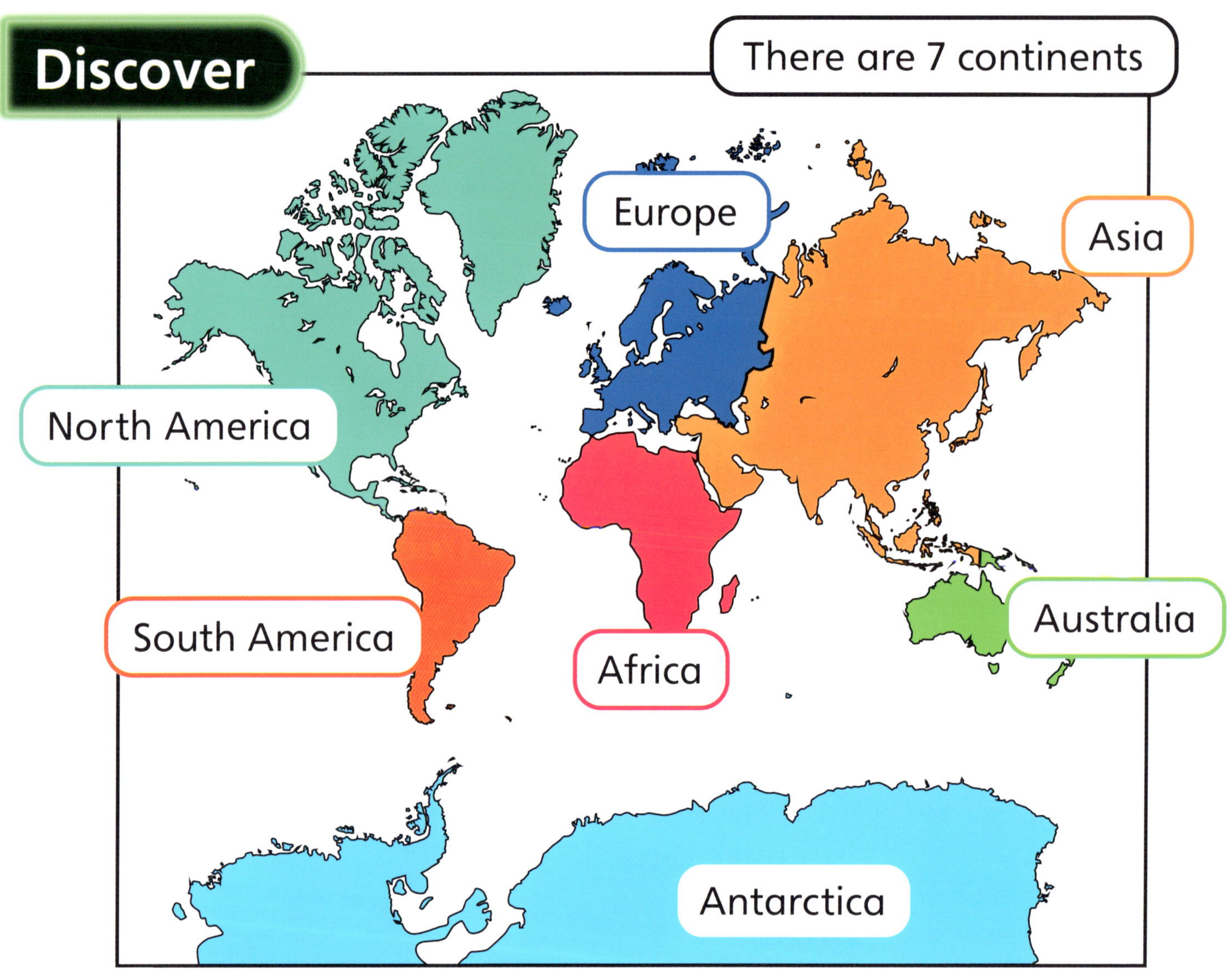

1 **a)** Complete the sentences.

The _____________ is the **whole**.

The _____________ are the parts.

world

continents

b) How many parts are there?

Share

a)

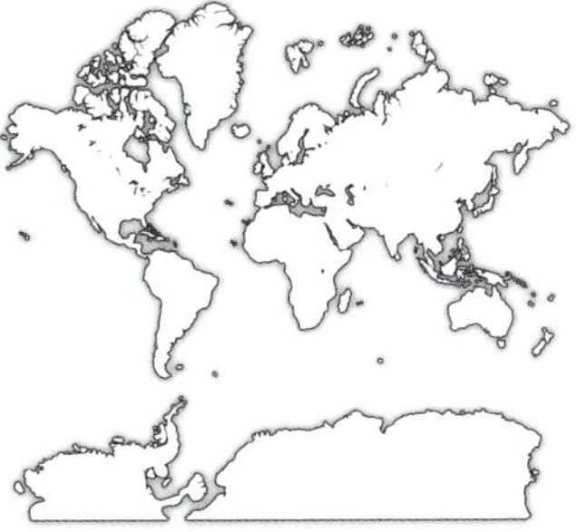

The world is the whole.

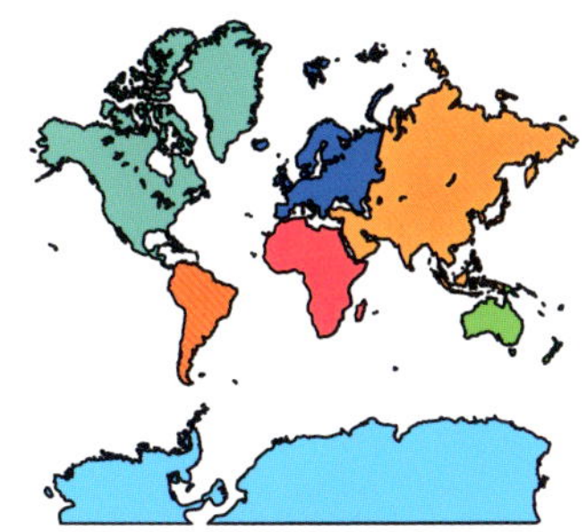

The continents are the parts.

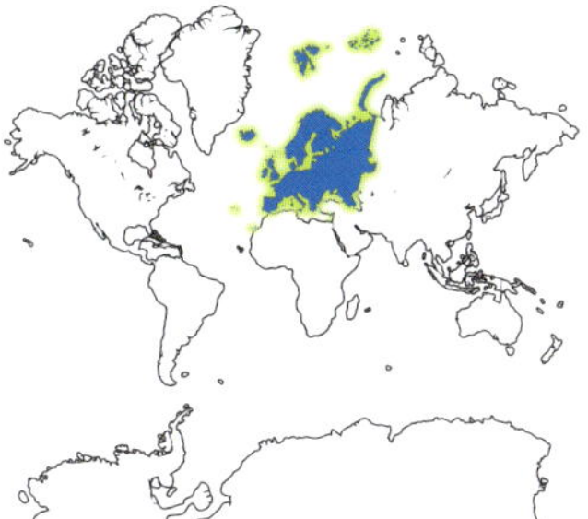

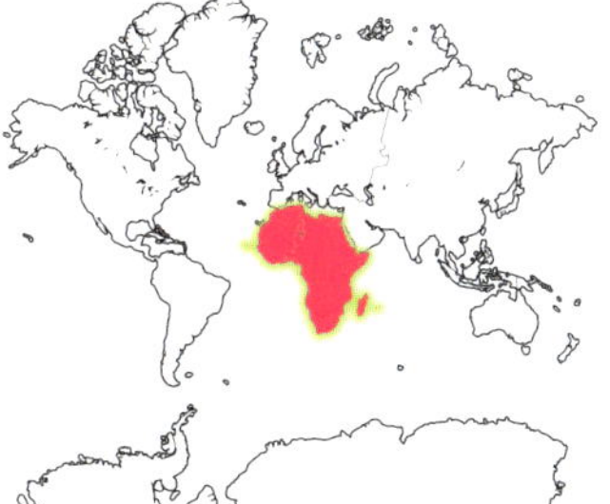

b) There are 7 continents, so there are 7 parts.

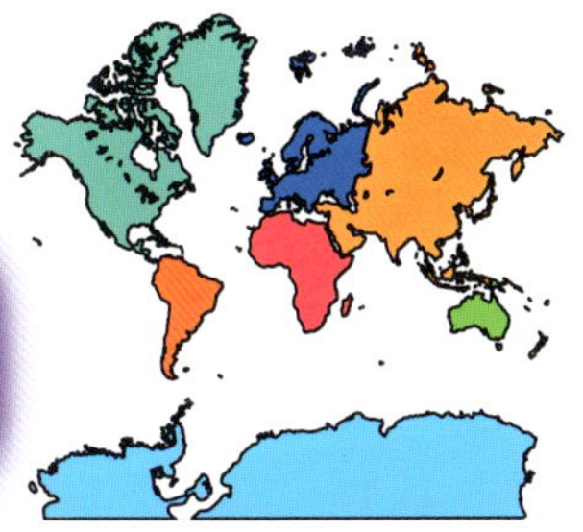

Think together

1. Complete the sentences.

   Here is the United Kingdom. There are 4 countries in the United Kingdom.

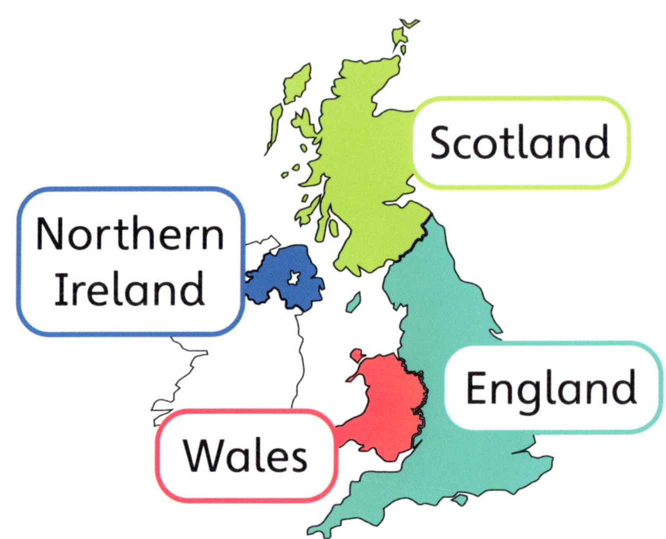

   a) The _____________ is the whole.

   b) _____________ is a part.

2. Here is an elephant.

   Complete the sentences in different ways.

   Use the words in the box.

   elephant
   trunk
   ear
   tail
   tusk
   eye

   a) The _____________ is the whole.

   b) The _____________ is a part.

3 Use the words 'whole' and 'part' to complete these sentences.

a)

The duck is the ______________ .

The beak is a ______________ .

b)

The sail is a ______________ .

The boat is the ______________ .

c)

The pizza is the ______________ .

The cheese is a ______________ .

→ **Practice book 2C p6**

Equal and unequal parts

Discover

1 **a)** Why is this not fair?

What could have been done differently?

b) Divide the cake fairly between 4 children.

Share

a)

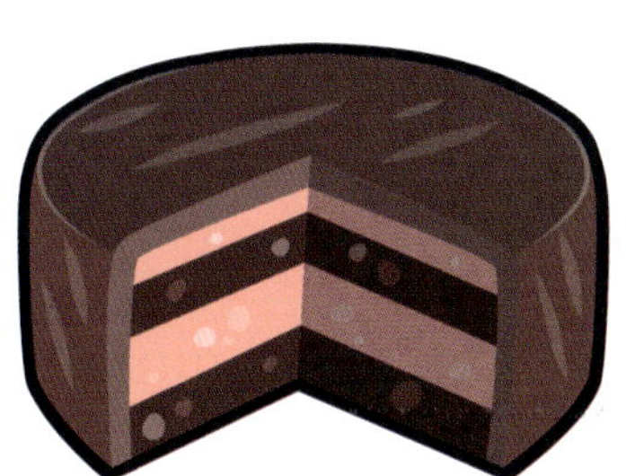

It is not fair because one of the parts is bigger than the other.

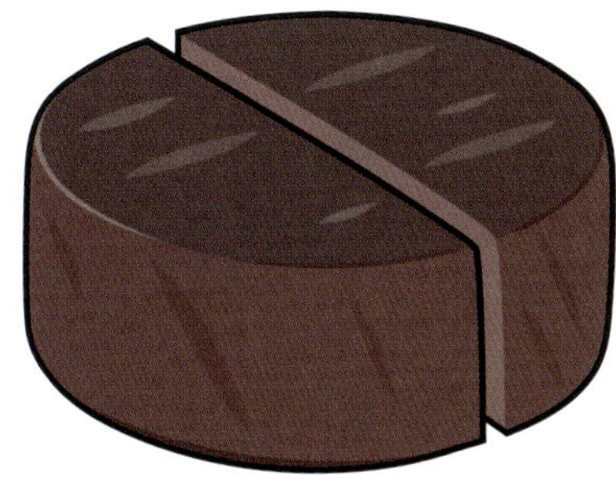

They could have cut the cake into 2 **equal parts**.

b)

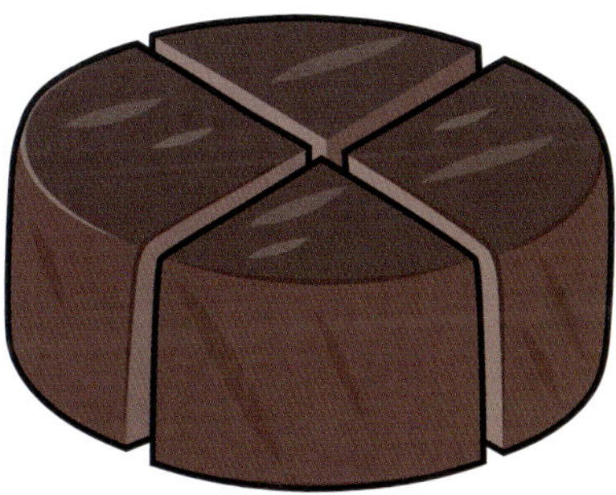

The cake has been cut into 4 equal parts.

Each child will get the same size piece.

Think together

1 Which show equal parts?

A

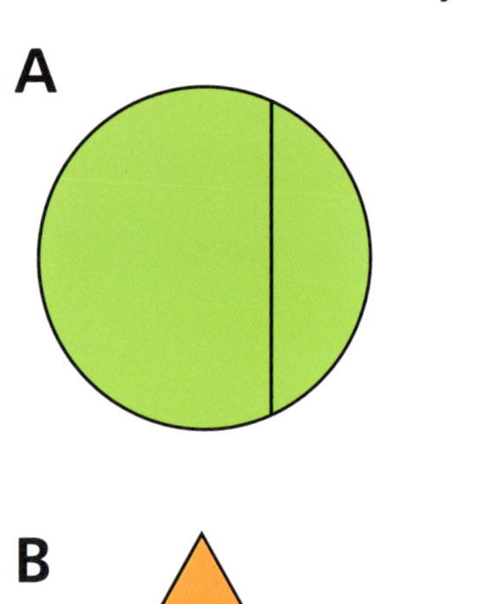

C

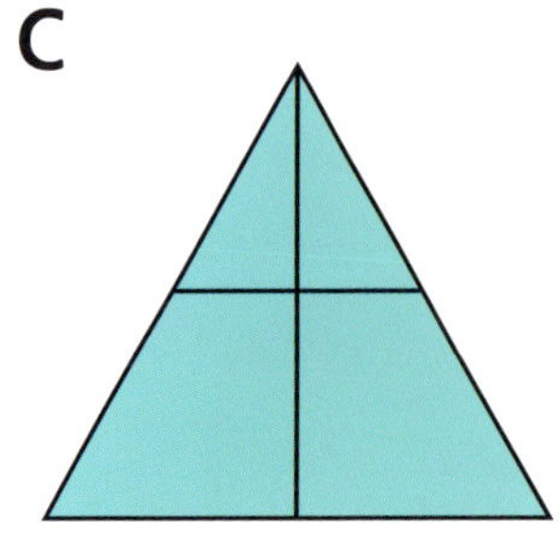

E

B

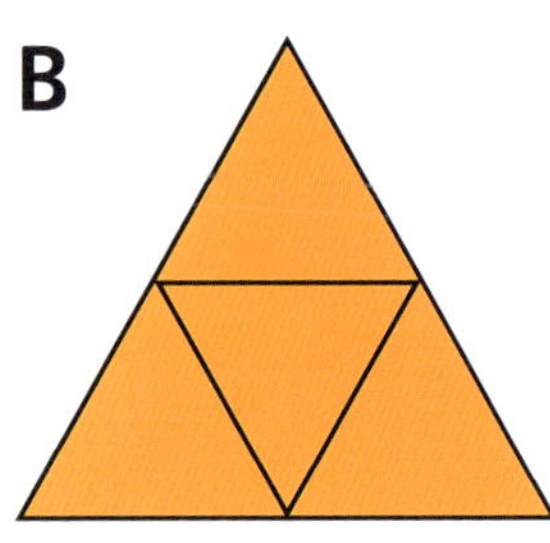

D

F

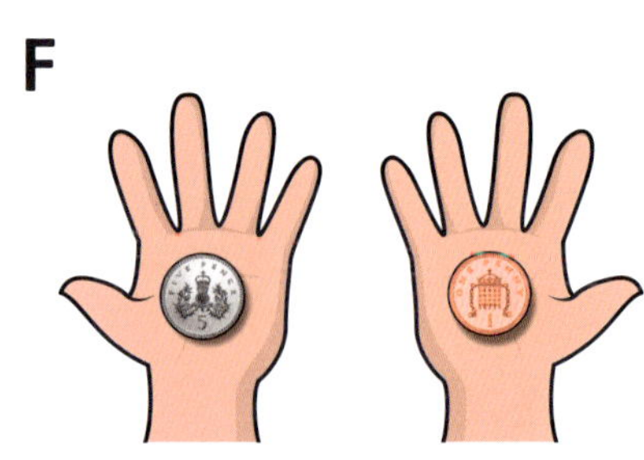

2 Which is the odd one out? Explain why.

A

B

C

The 'odd one out' is the picture that is different to the others in some way.

3 How could you make equal groups of children?

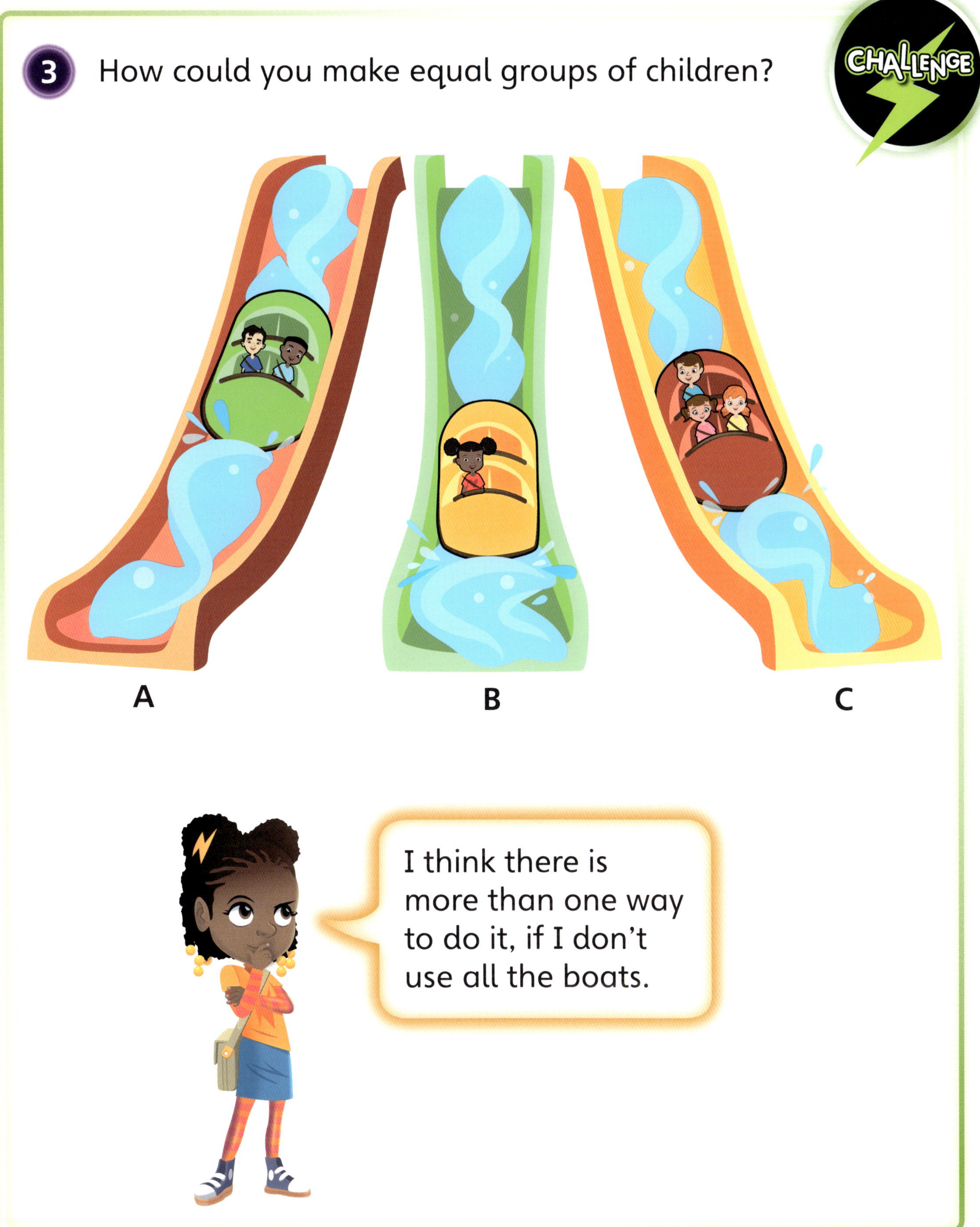

→ Practice book 2C p9

Recognise a half

Discover

1 a) Fold a sheet of paper in half, then open it up. What do you see?

b) Discuss with a partner what you know about $\frac{1}{2}$.

Recognise a half

Share

a)

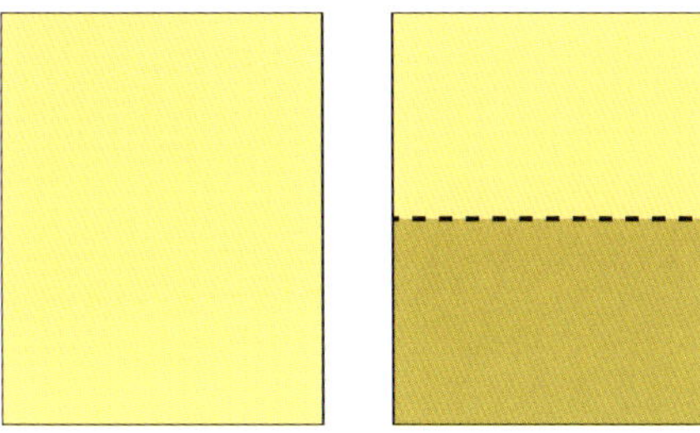

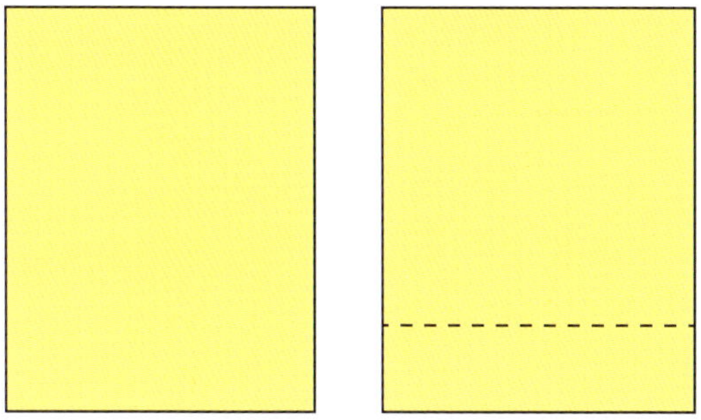

b) The **denominator** is the total number of equal parts.

The denominator of $\frac{1}{2}$ is 2.

There are two equal parts.

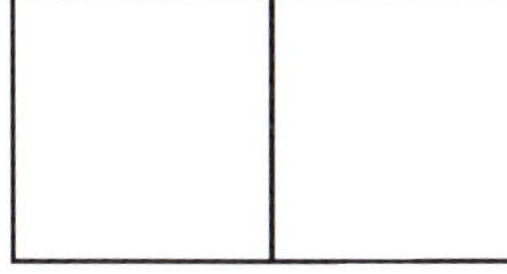

The **numerator** is how many of the equal parts there are.

The numerator of $\frac{1}{2}$ is 1.
It is one of two equal parts.

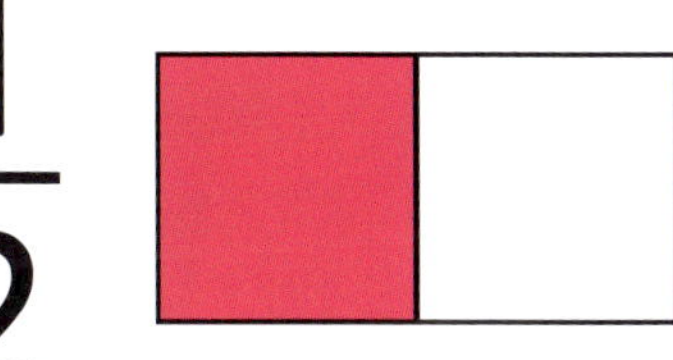

Think together

1. Fold a square to make halves.
   Try this 3 different ways.

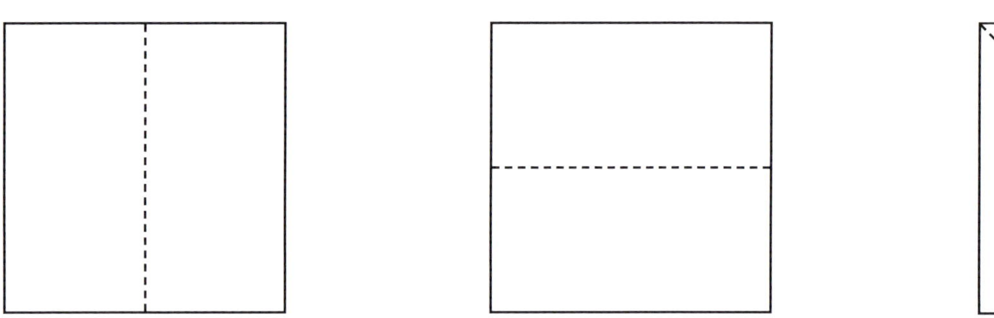

2. Draw 3 circles.
   Split each circle into two halves.
   Shade one half of each circle.

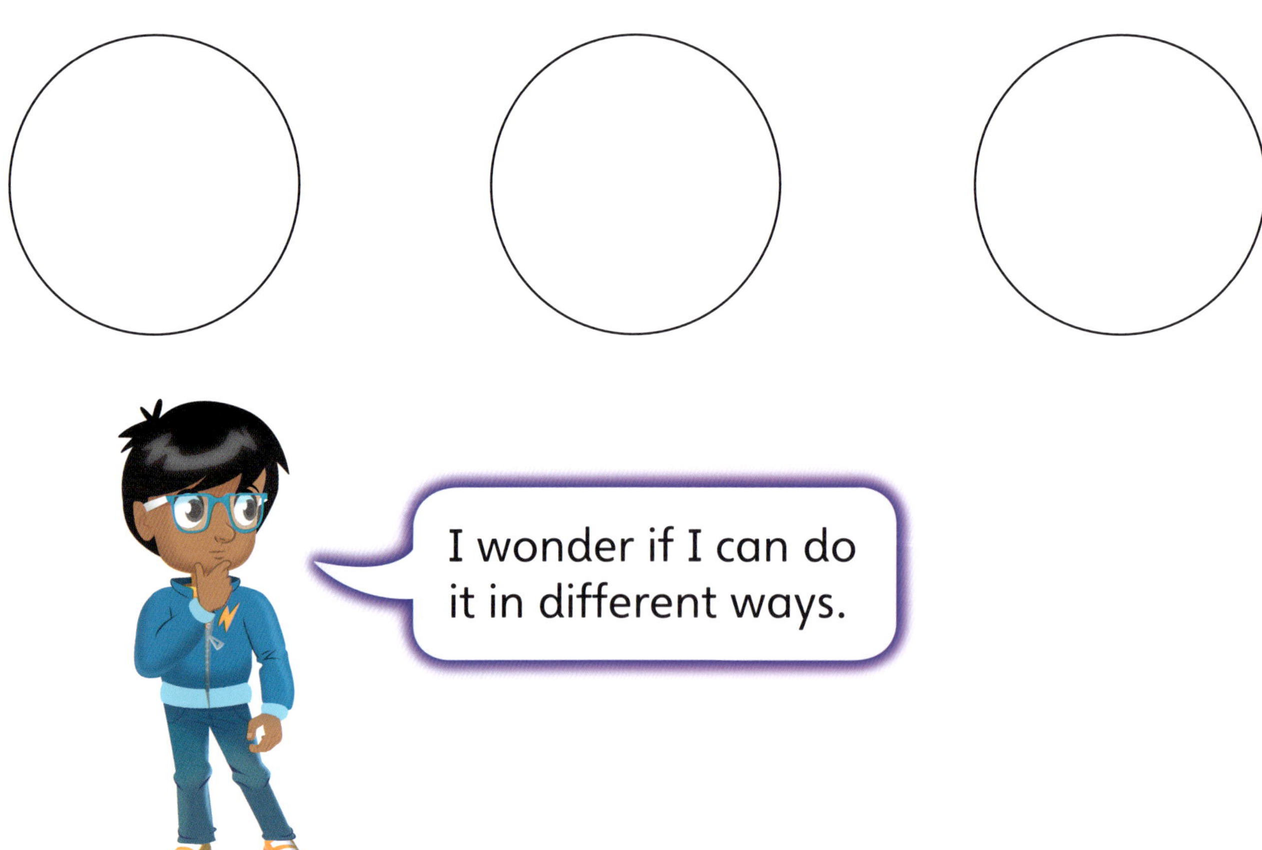

3 **a)** Who has run exactly half-way?

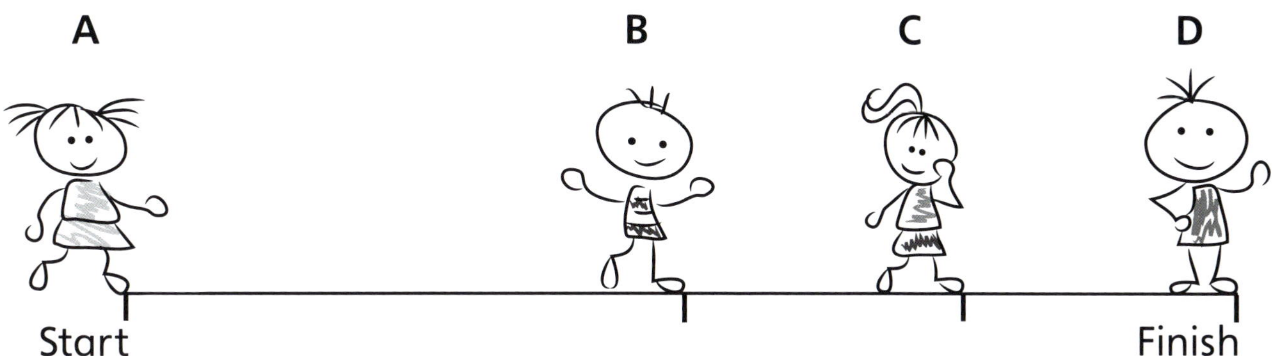

b) Which arrow points half-way along the line?

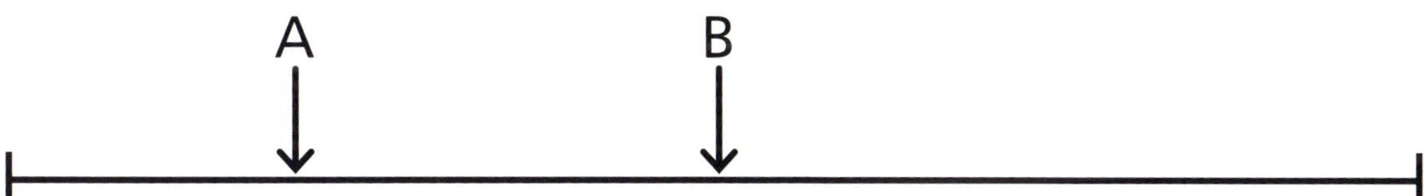

19

→ Practice book 2C p12

Find a half

Discover

1   **a)**   Make 2 equal teams.

      b)   What is $\frac{1}{2}$ of 10?

Share

a) There are 10 players in total.

Each team has 5 players.

b)

$2 \times 5 = 10$

$\frac{1}{2}$ of 10 is 5.

Think together

1. Find half of each number.

a) 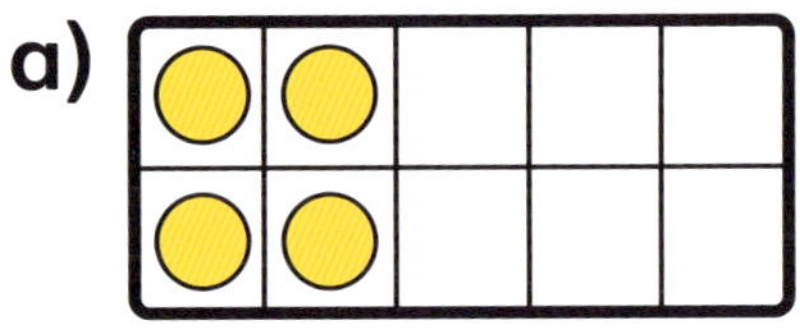

$\frac{1}{2}$ of 4 is ☐.

b) 

$\frac{1}{2}$ of 6 is ☐.

c) 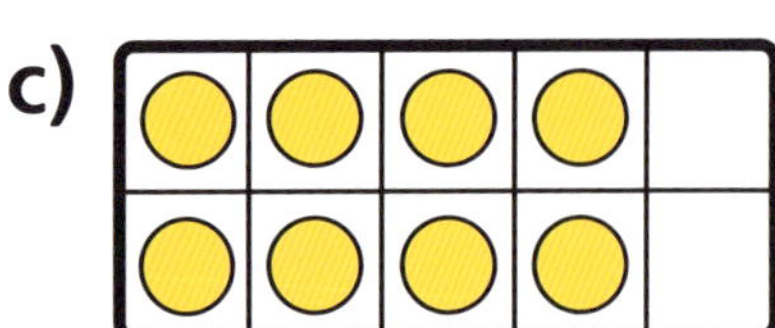

$\frac{1}{2}$ of 8 is ☐.

2. Find $\frac{1}{2}$ of 14.

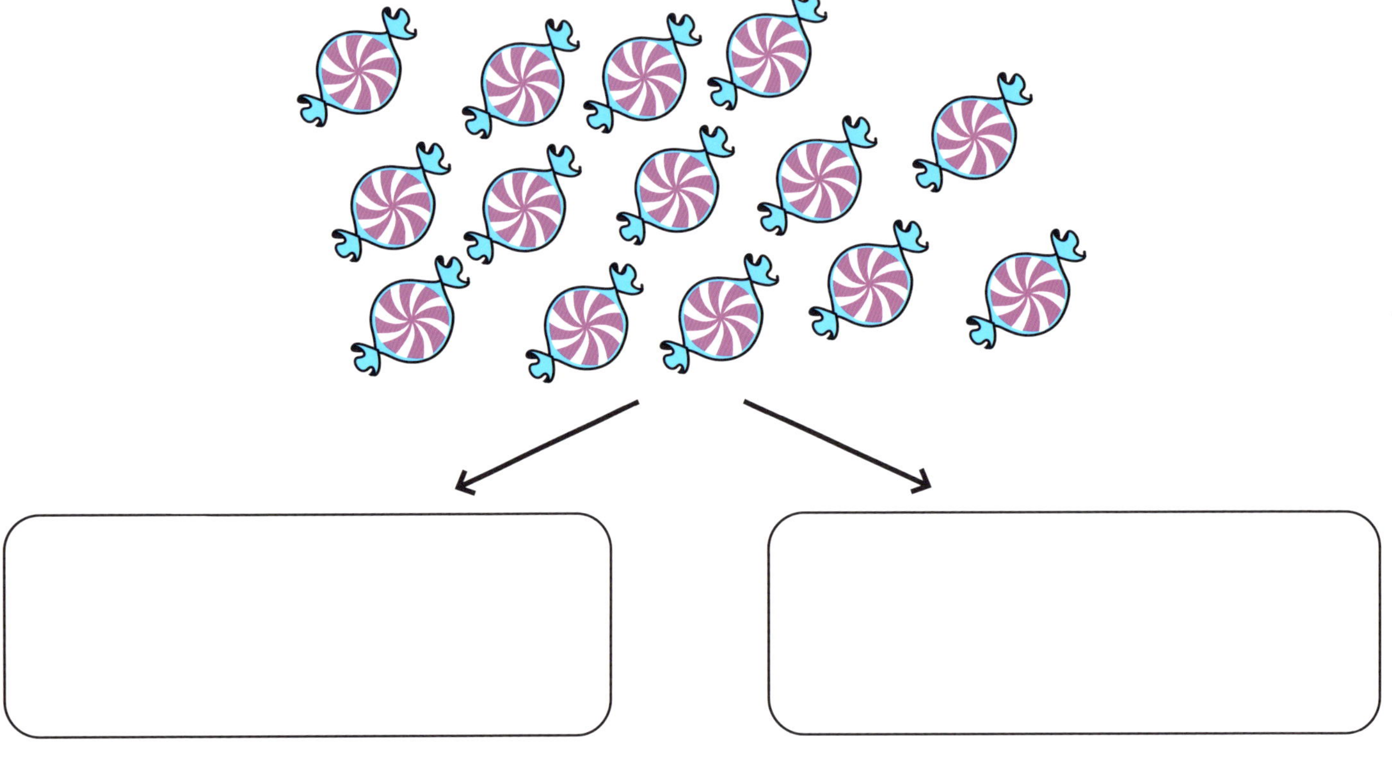

3 a)

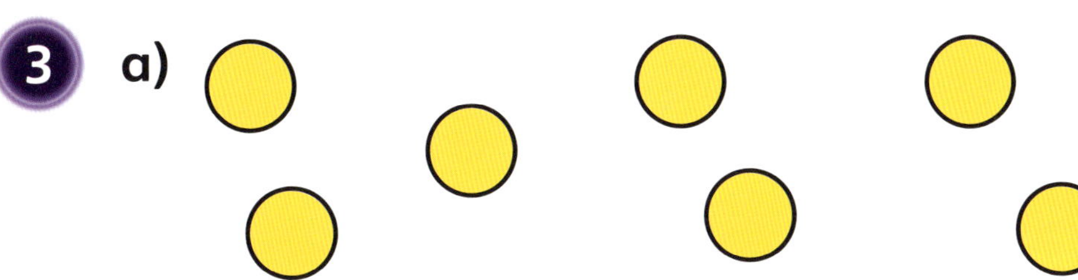

Sort the counters into two halves.

What do you notice?

b)

1	2	3	4	5	6	7	8	9	10
11	12	13	14	15	16	17	18	19	20

Which of these numbers can you share into two halves?

23

Recognise a quarter

Discover

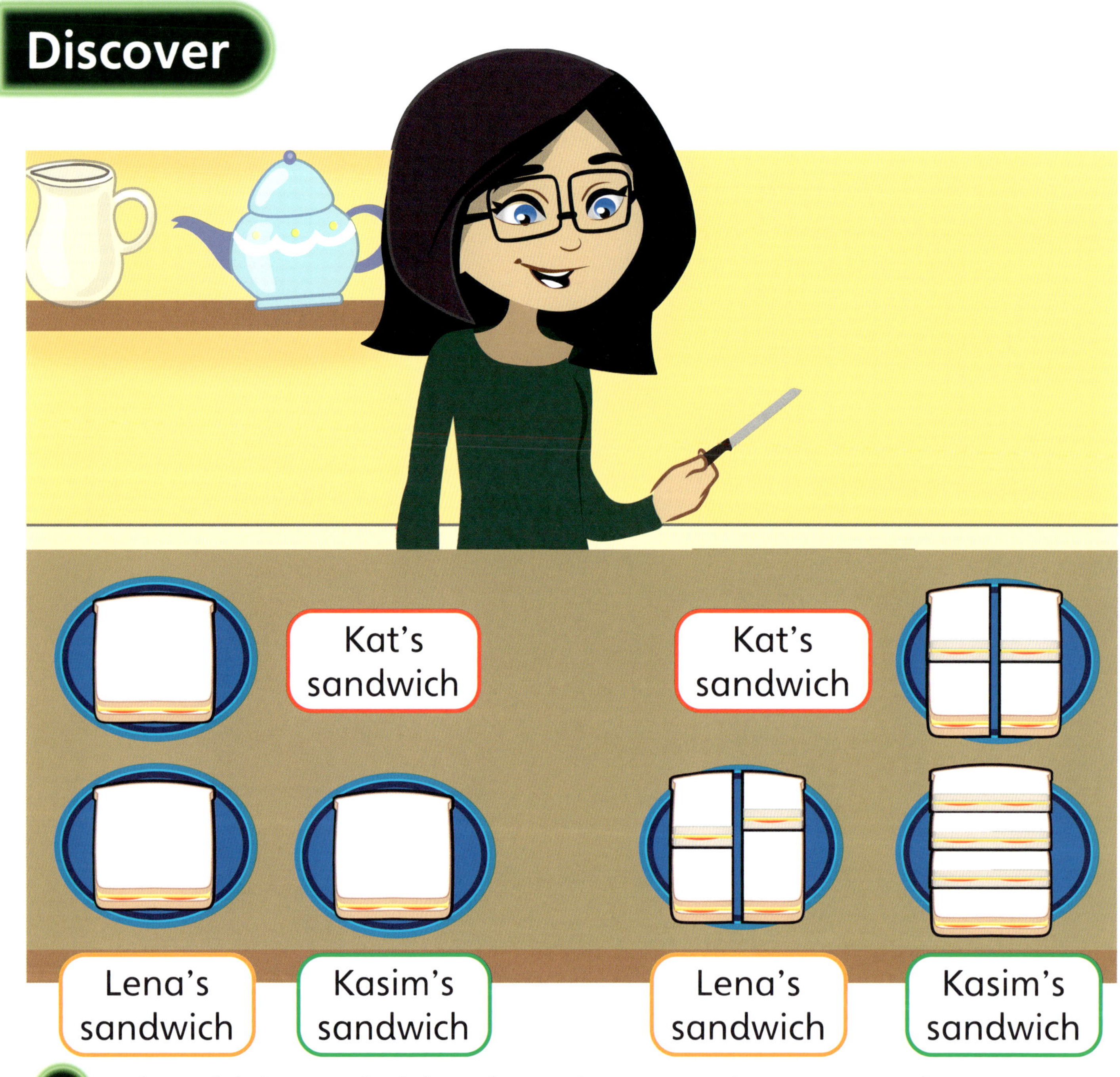

1 **a)** Which sandwiches have been cut into 4 equal parts?

Which sandwich is not cut into 4 equal parts?

b) Can you show another way to cut a square into 4 equal parts?

Share

a)

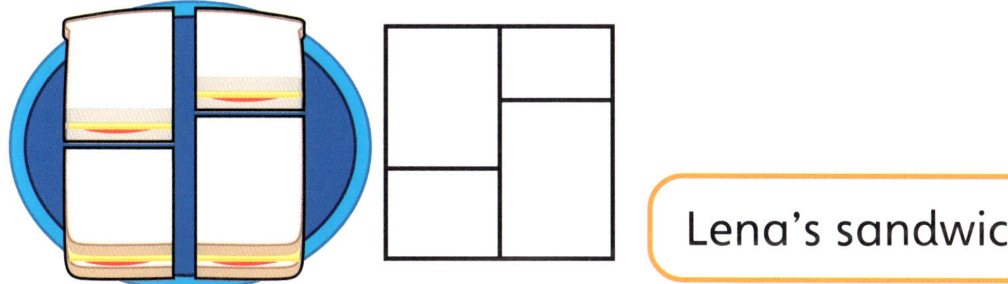

Kat's sandwich   Kasim's sandwich

The whole has been split into four equal parts.

Each part is one quarter.

Lena's sandwich

The whole has been split into four unequal parts.

The parts are not quarters.

b) Here are two more ways to split a square into quarters.

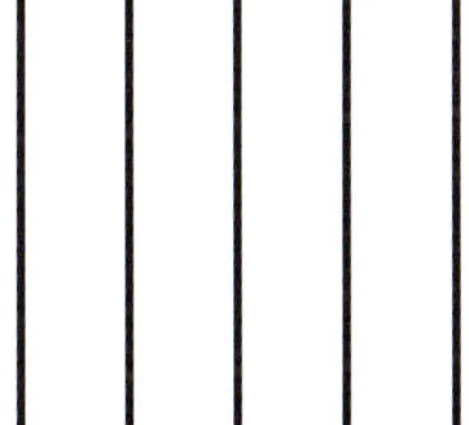 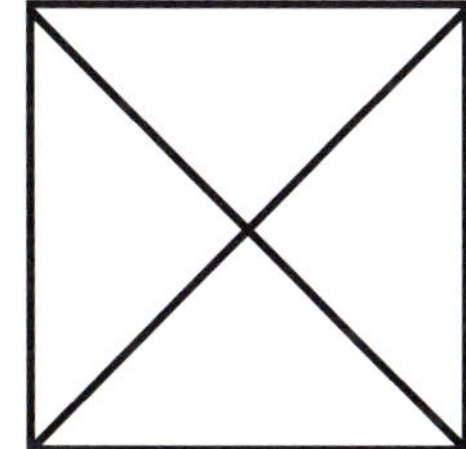

Think together

1

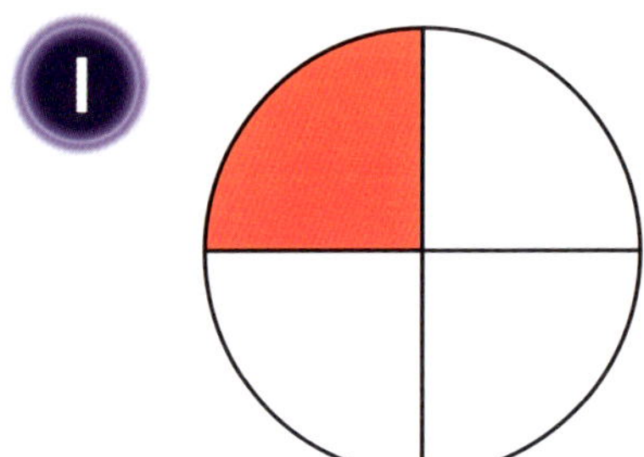

The whole has been split into four equal parts.
Each part is one quarter.

Practise writing $\frac{1}{4}$. Follow these steps.

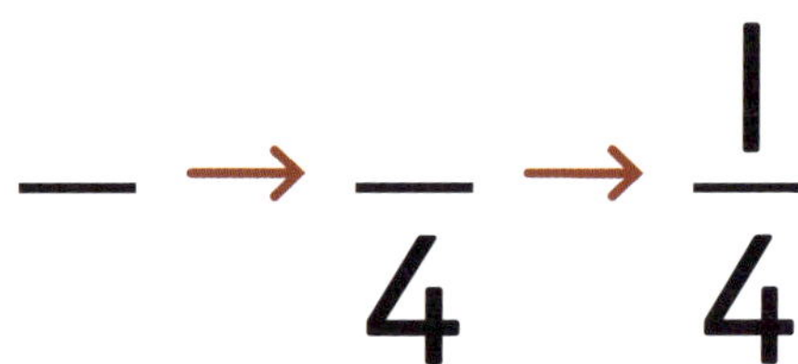

Discuss with a partner the meaning of each step.

2 Copy each shape. Shade one quarter of each shape.

a)

b)

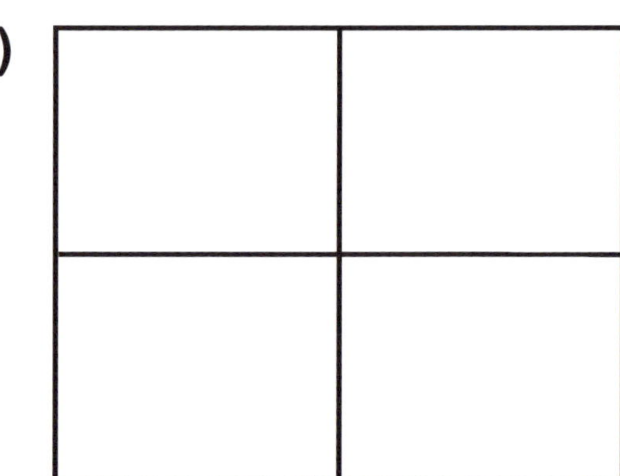

3 What do you notice about the quarters on each strip?

27

Find a quarter

Discover

Ola

Filip

Em

Josh

1 **a)** Can the counters be split into 4 equal groups?

b) How many counters will each child get?

Share

a)

The counters can be split into 4 equal groups.

b)

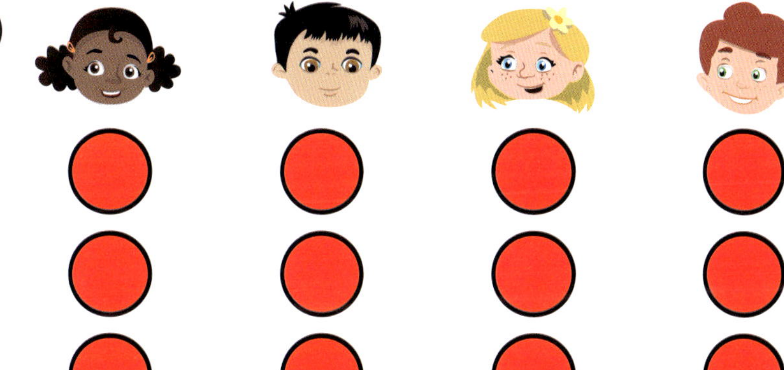

$\frac{1}{4}$ of 12 counters is 3 counters.

Each child will get 3 counters.

Think together

1

Share the counters between the children.

How many counters will each child get?

2 Mr Singh is sharing pencils between 4 pots.

How many pencils will be in each pot?

3 **a)** Lucy has 13 cubes.

She wants to split them into quarters.

She shares them into 4 groups.

   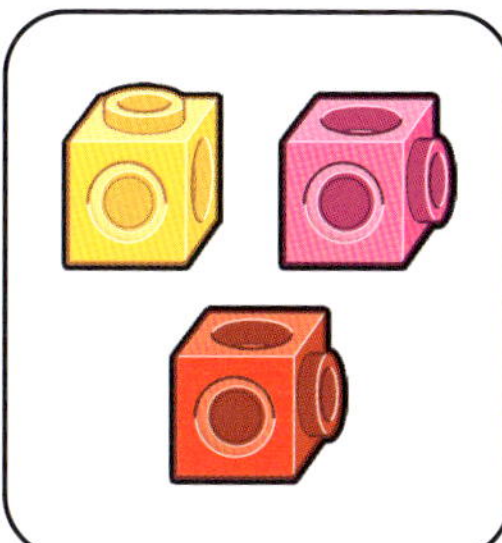

$\frac{1}{4}$ of 13 = 3

Is Lucy correct? Explain your answer.

b) Harry has 10 cubes.

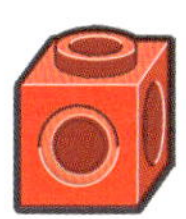    

How many more cubes does he need to be able to split them into quarters?

→ **Practice book 2C p21**

Thirds

1 **a)** What fraction does the flag of Monaco show?

What fraction does the flag of Mauritius show?

Write both fractions down.

b) What fraction are the flags of Chad and Germany split into?

Write the answer down.

Share

a) The flag of Monaco is split into 2 equal parts.
Each part is one half.

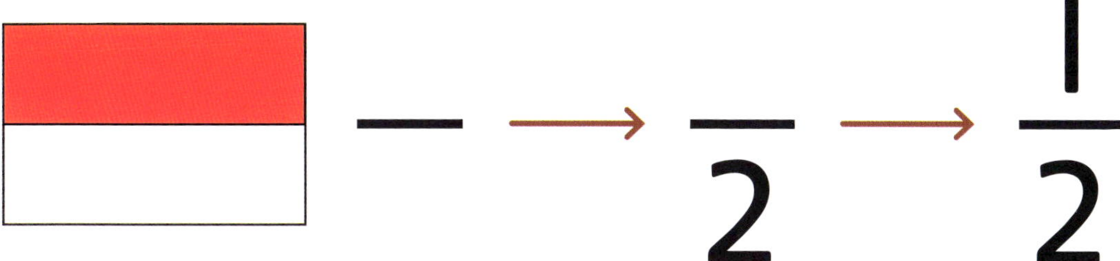

The flag of Mauritius is split into 4 equal parts.
Each part is one quarter.

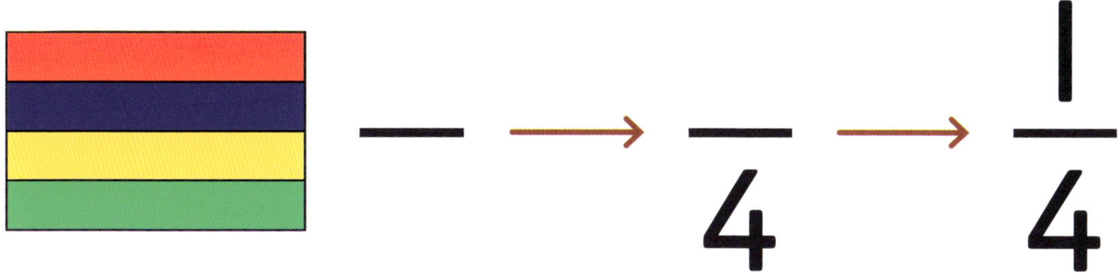

b) Each flag is split into 3 equal parts.

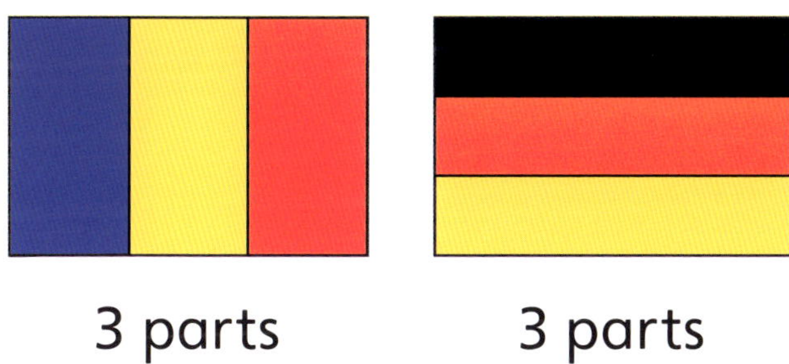

3 parts   3 parts

The whole is split
into 3 equal parts.
Each part is one third.

Think together

1 Class 2 have been making their own flags.

Which flags have been split into thirds?

2 Which circles show $\frac{1}{3}$ shaded?

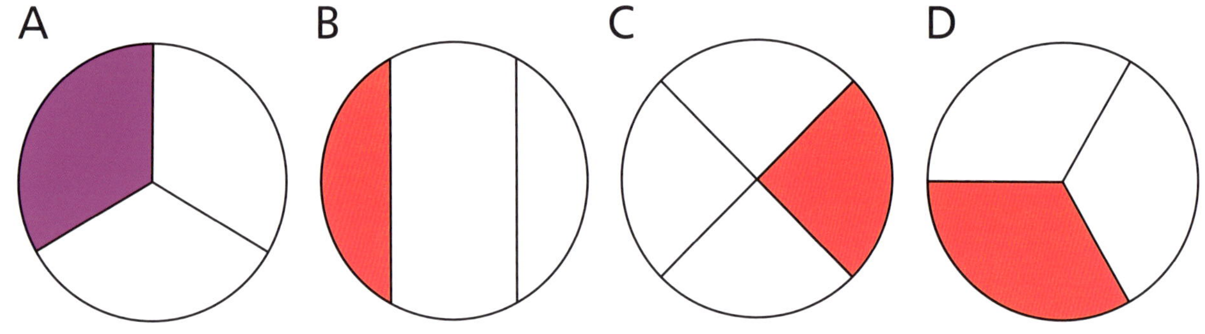

3 **a)** Find $\frac{1}{3}$ of 6.

b) What is $\frac{1}{3}$ of 12 strawberries?

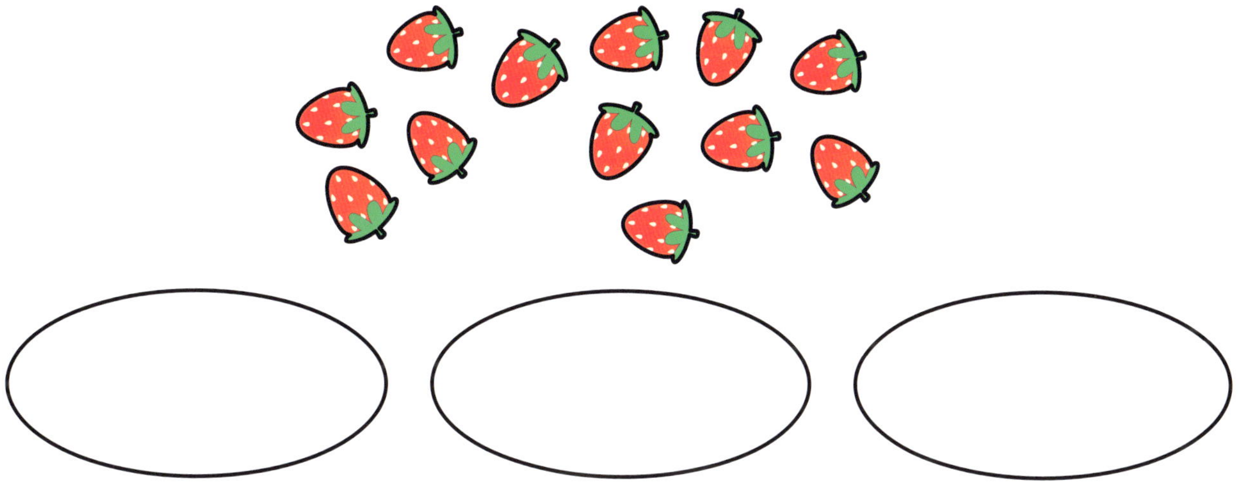

→ **Practice book 2C p24**

Find the whole

Discover

1 **a)** Danny has sorted his cubes into quarters.

How many cubes are there in each quarter?

How many cubes make up the whole?

b) Meg sorts her cubes into quarters.

There are 5 cubes in each quarter. How many cubes make up the whole?

Share

a)

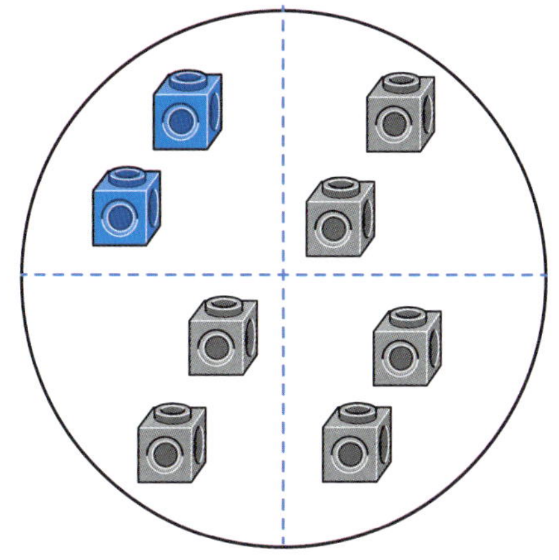

There are 2 cubes in each quarter.

8 cubes make up the whole.

b) There are 5 cubes in each quarter.
20 cubes make up the whole.

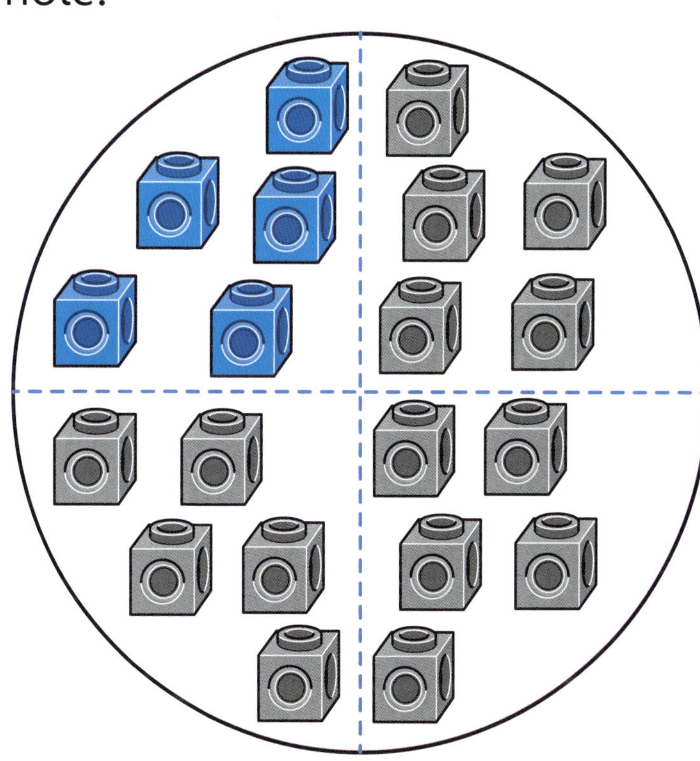

Think together

1 One half is 5 cubes.

What is the whole?

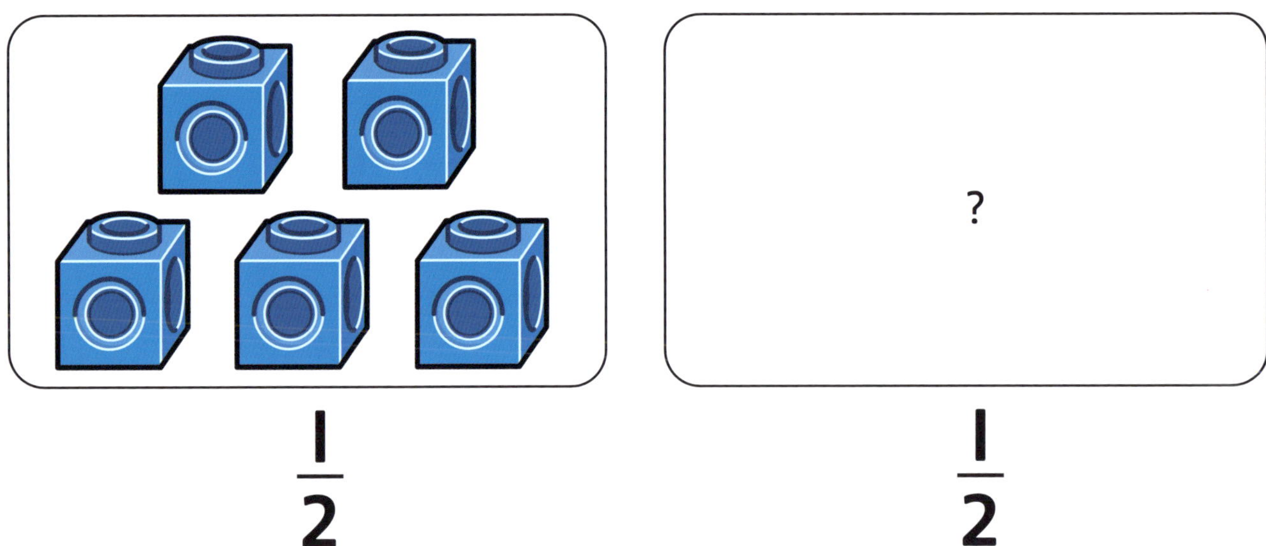

$\dfrac{1}{2}$ $\dfrac{1}{2}$

2 One third is 10 counters.

What is the whole?

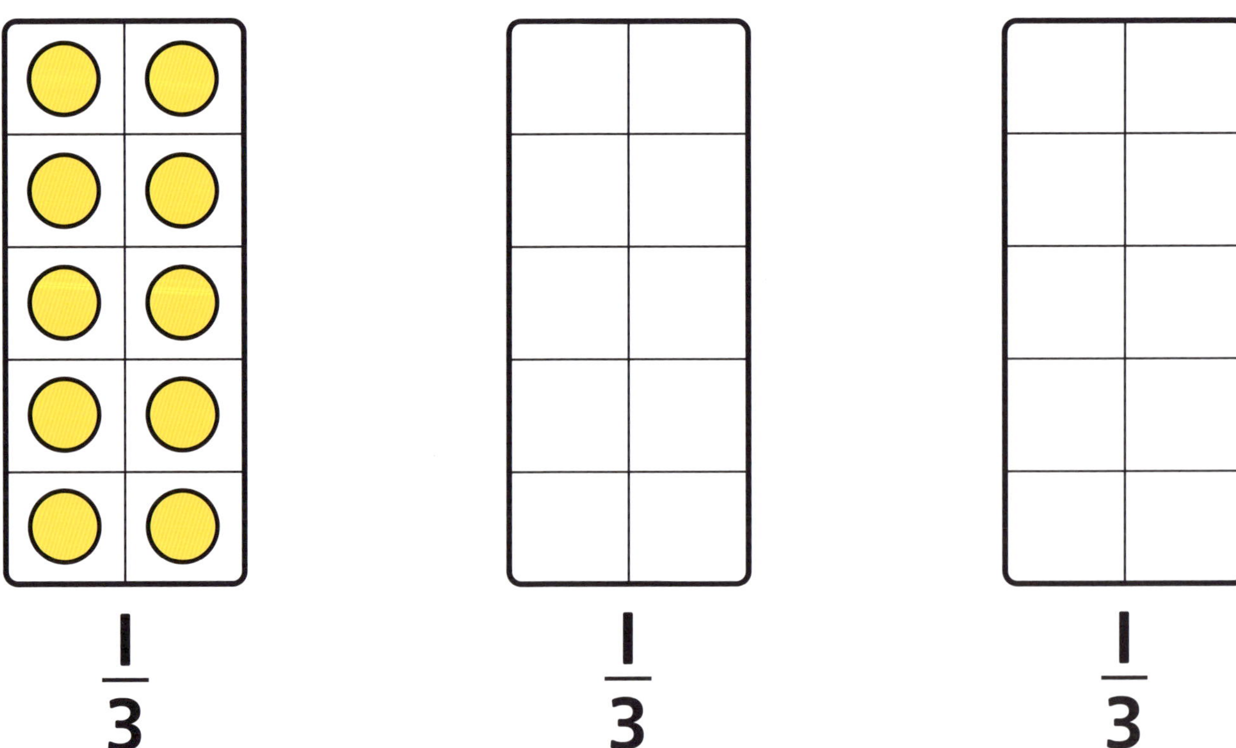

$\dfrac{1}{3}$ $\dfrac{1}{3}$ $\dfrac{1}{3}$

3 

a) What is the same and what is different about these number sentences?

$\frac{1}{2}$ of 10 = ☐

$\frac{1}{2}$ of ☐ = 10

b) Solve these calculations.

$\frac{1}{2}$ of 6 = ☐ $\frac{1}{4}$ of 8 = ☐

$\frac{1}{2}$ of ☐ = 6 $\frac{1}{4}$ of ☐ = 8

→ **Practice book 2C p27**

Unit and non-unit fractions

Discover

1 **a)** What fractions are the kites split into?

b) What fraction of each kite is plain yellow?

Share

a)

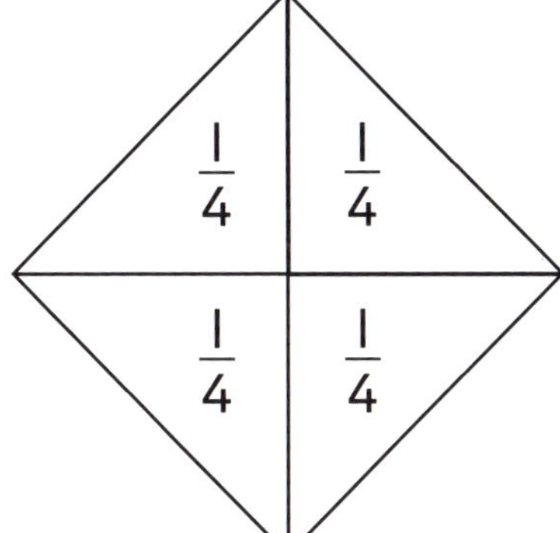

Each kite is split into 4 equal parts.

Each part is one quarter of the whole.

b)

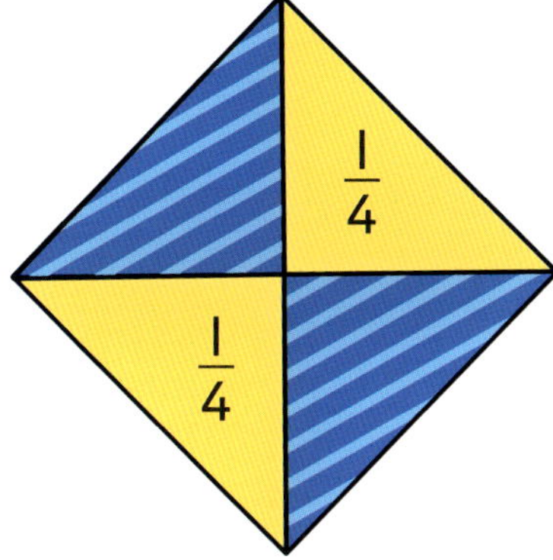

Two quarters are plain yellow. $\dfrac{2}{4}$

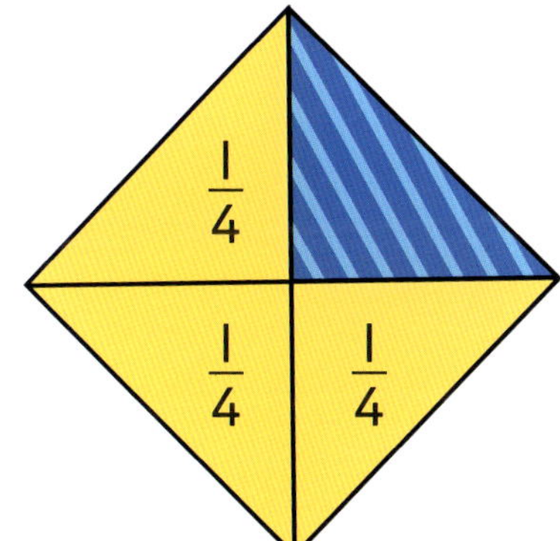

Three quarters are plain yellow. $\dfrac{3}{4}$

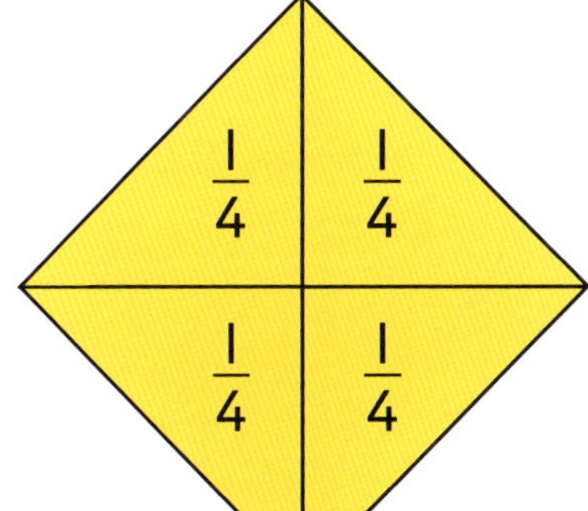

Four quarters are plain yellow. $\dfrac{4}{4}$

Think together

1. Discuss the numerator and denominator of this fraction.

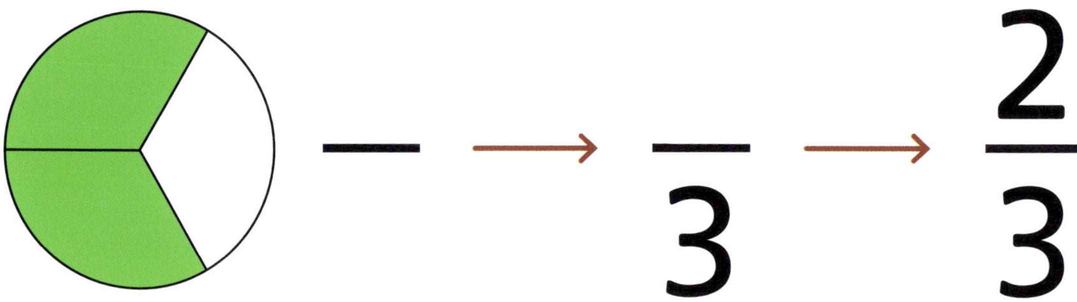

$$\_ \longrightarrow \frac{}{3} \longrightarrow \frac{2}{3}$$

2. Draw a picture to show halves.

Shade $\frac{1}{2}$ on your picture.

Now shade another $\frac{1}{2}$.

Write the fraction for two halves.

What do you notice?

3 **a)** Fold a strip into halves.

Label each half with a unit fraction.

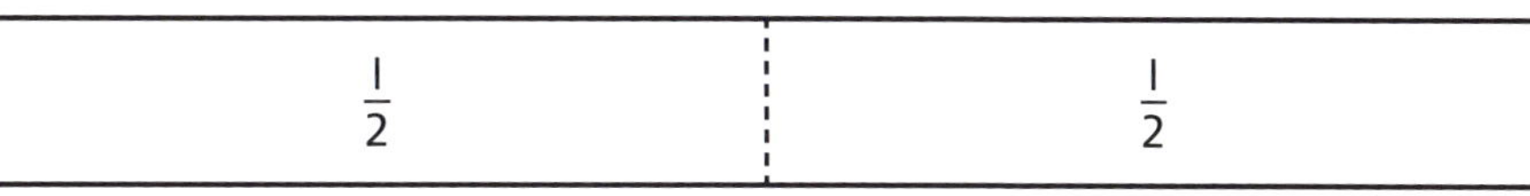

Shade one half.
What fraction have
you shaded?

Shade the other half.
What fraction have
you shaded now?

b) Fold a strip into quarters.

Label each quarter with a unit fraction.

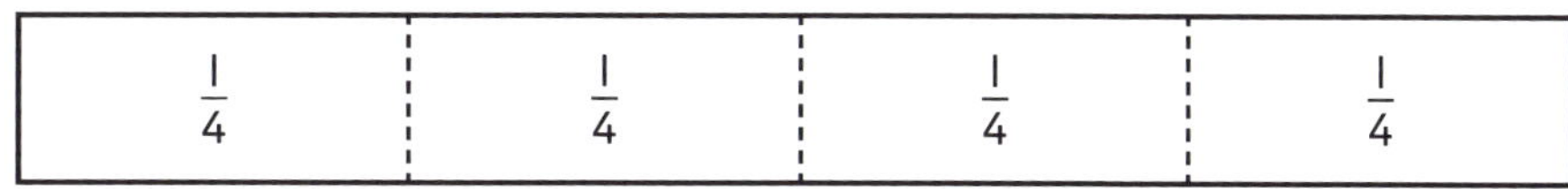

Shade one quarter.
What fraction have you shaded?

Shade one more quarter.
What fraction have you shaded now?

Shade one more quarter.
What fraction have you shaded now?

Shade one more quarter.
What fraction have you shaded altogether?

43

Recognise the equivalence of a half and two quarters

Discover

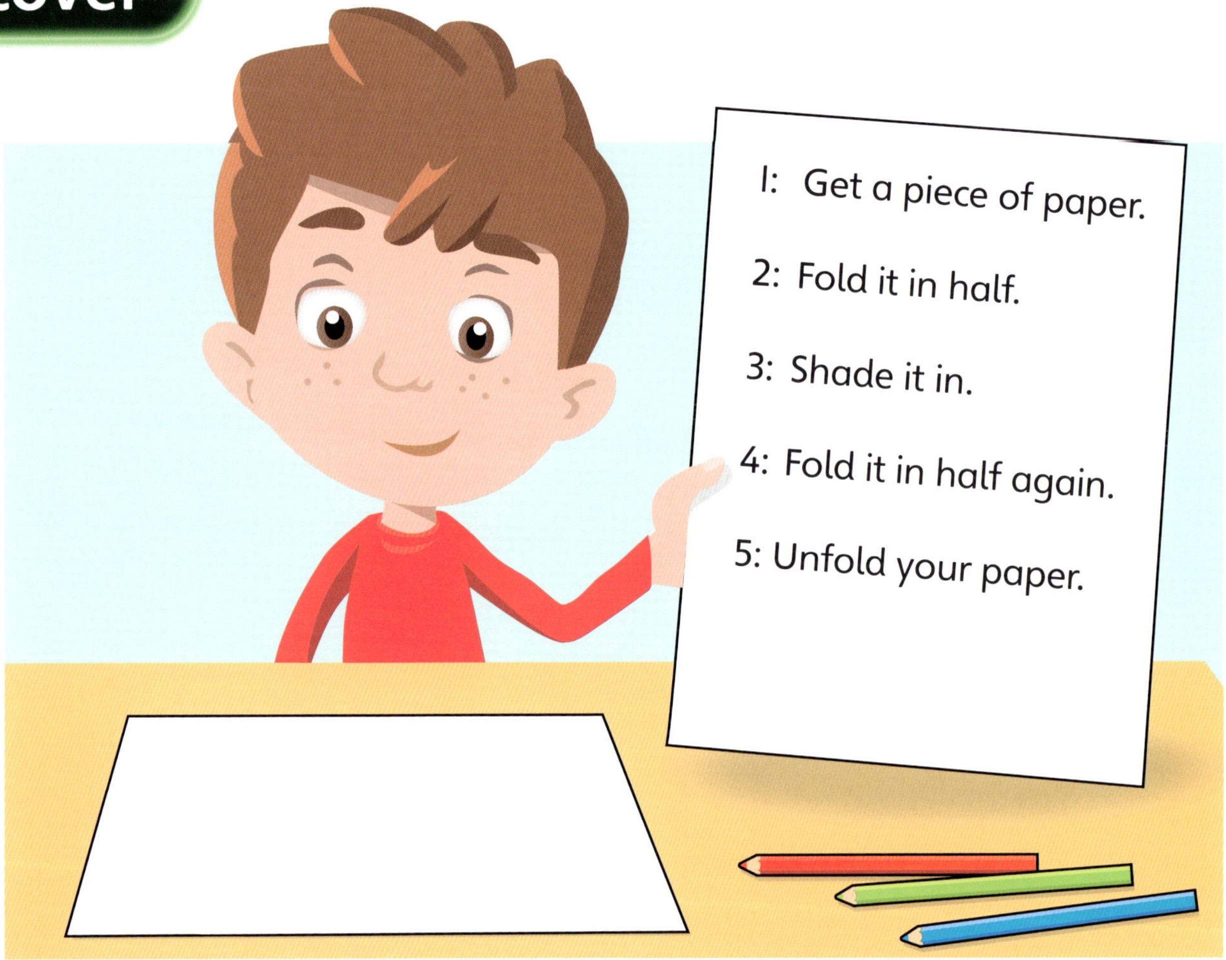

1 **a)** Follow the instructions. What do you notice?

What fraction is shaded?

b) Does the same thing happen when you fold and shade these shapes?

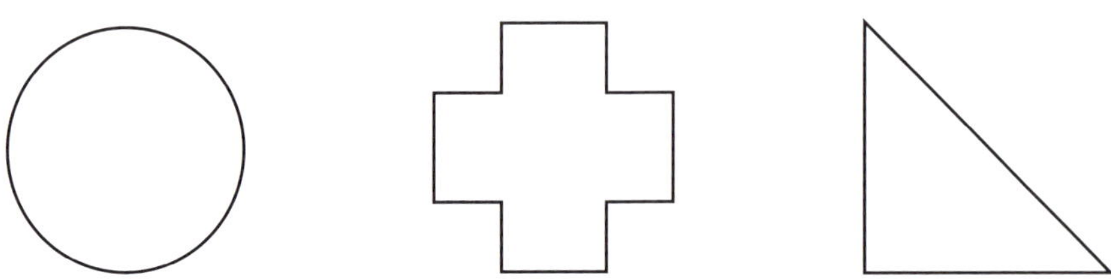

Share

a) Step 1

Step 2

Step 3

Step 4

Step 5

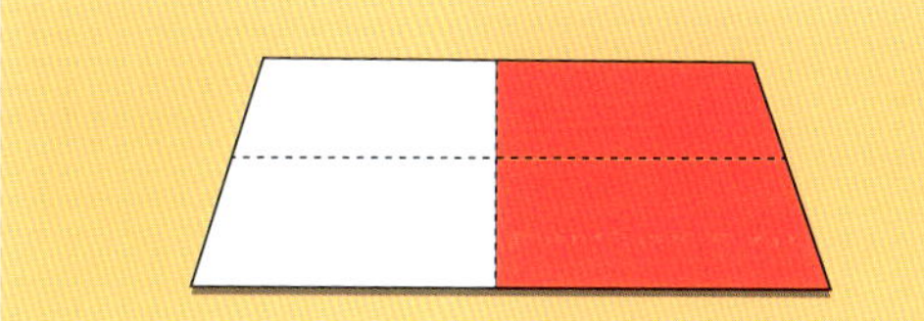

I checked by cutting $\frac{1}{2}$ out and placing it on top of $\frac{2}{4}$. They were the same size!

The paper is now divided into quarters.

$\frac{1}{2}$ of the paper is shaded. $\frac{1}{2}$ and $\frac{2}{4}$ are **equivalent**.

b) It is the same with the other shapes.

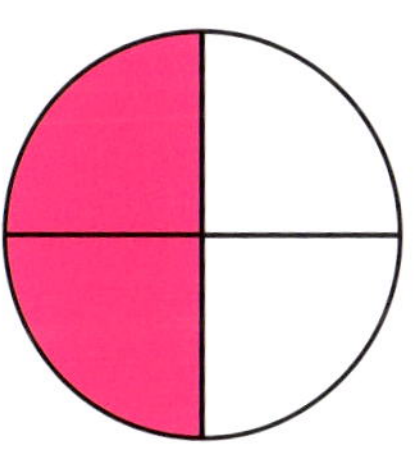

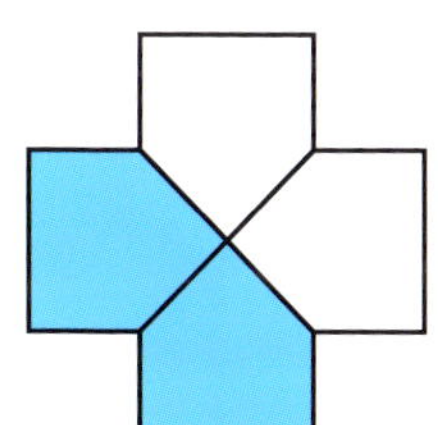

I explored lots of different ways to show halves and quarters.

Think together

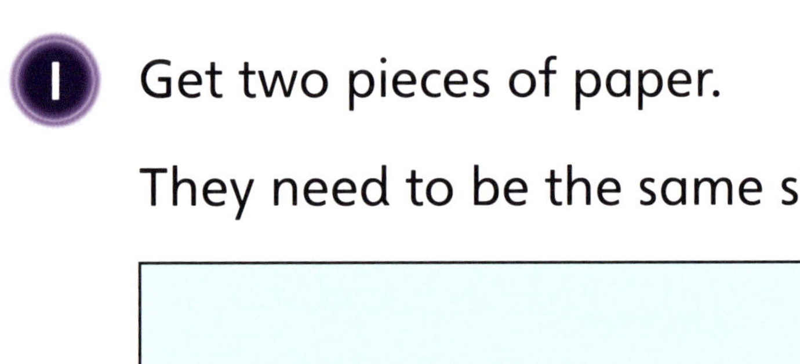

1 Get two pieces of paper.

They need to be the same size.

How can you split the strips of paper
to show that $\frac{1}{2}$ and $\frac{2}{4}$ are equal?

2 **a)** Find $\frac{1}{2}$ of 8.

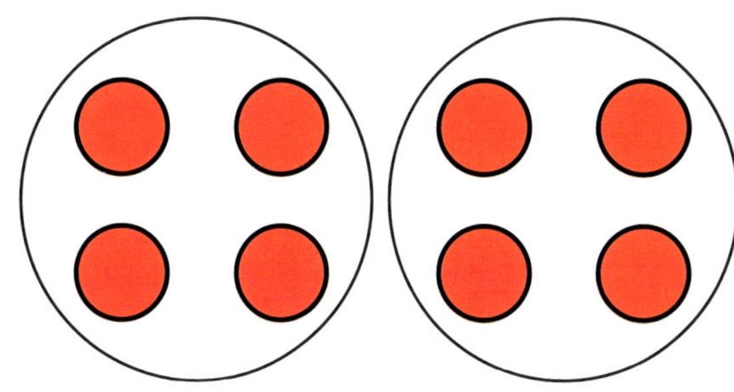

b) Find $\frac{1}{4}$ of 8.

What is $\frac{2}{4}$ of 8?

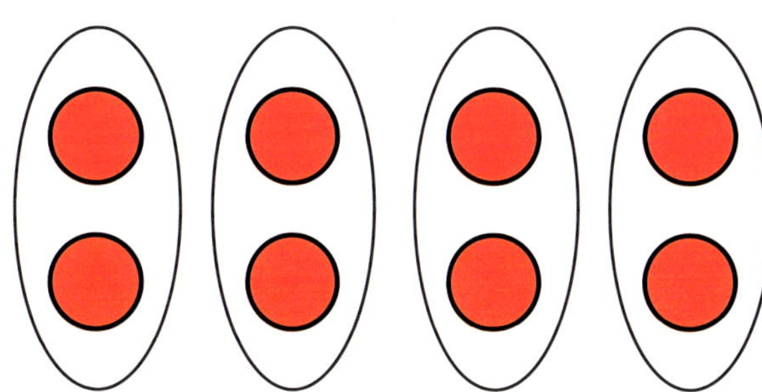

What do you notice about your answers? Why do you think this is the case?

3 Tami says that this bar model can help her solve $\frac{2}{4}$ of 12.

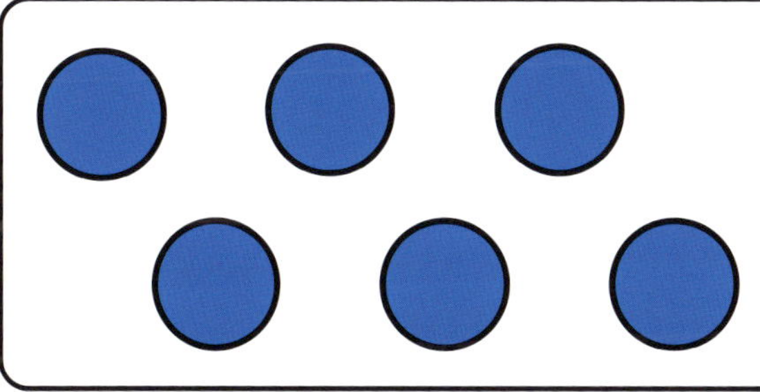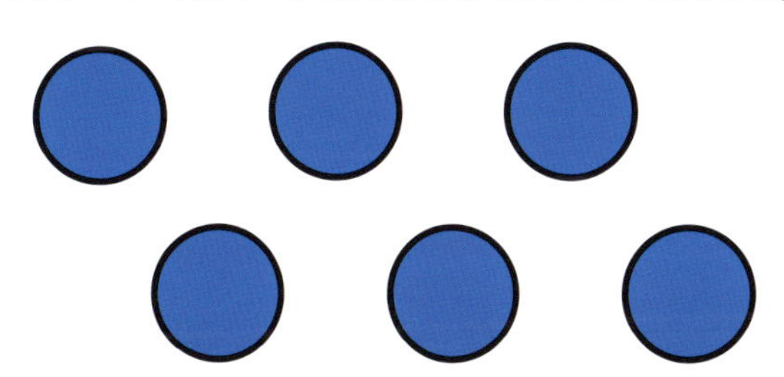

Do you agree?

Explain why.

→ Practice book 2C p33

Recognise three quarters

Discover

1 **a)** What fraction of the pizza has mushrooms?

b) What fraction of the pizza does **not** have any mushrooms?

Share

a) There are 4 equal slices of pizza.

Each slice is one quarter of the pizza.

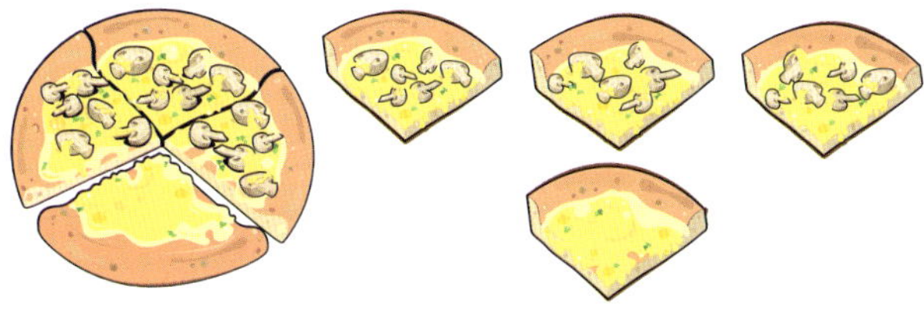

3 out of 4 of the equal parts have mushrooms.

3 out of 4 equal parts can be written as $\frac{3}{4}$ or **three quarters**.

$\frac{3}{4}$ of the pizza has mushrooms.

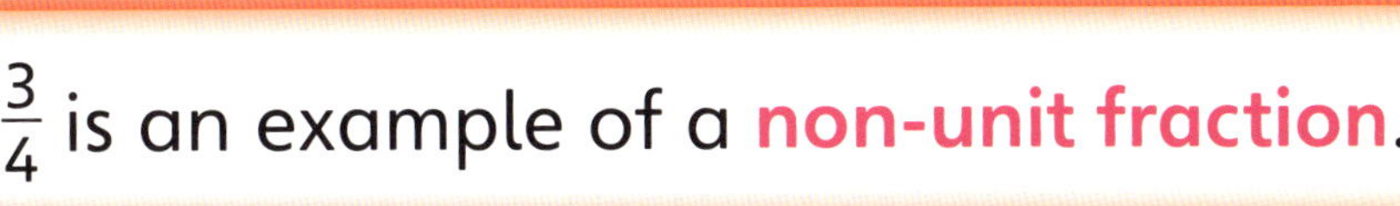

b) 1 out of 4 equal parts does not have any mushrooms.

1 out of 4 equal parts is written as $\frac{1}{4}$ or one quarter.

$\frac{1}{4}$ of the pizza does not have any mushrooms.

Think together

1 Gino has 8 slices of pizza.

He shares them equally between 4 people.

a) How many slices does he give to 1 person?

b) How many slices does he give to 3 people?

2 Which shapes show $\frac{3}{4}$ shaded?

a)
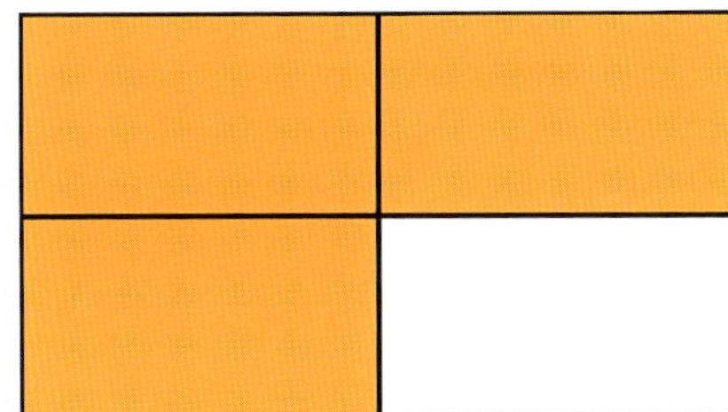

c)
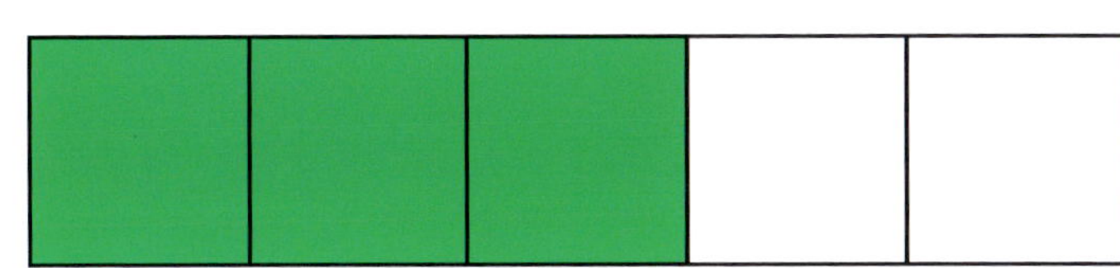

b)
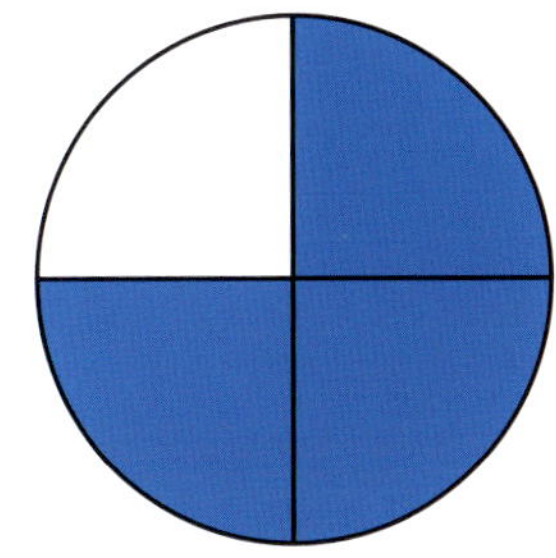

d)
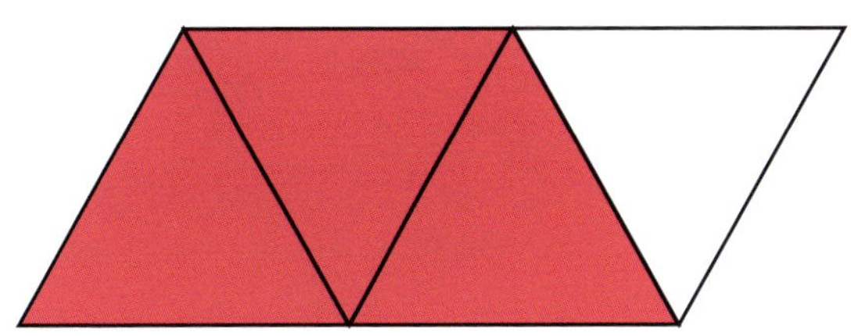

3 What fraction of the shape is shaded?

51

→ Practice book 2C p36

Count in fractions up to a whole

Discover

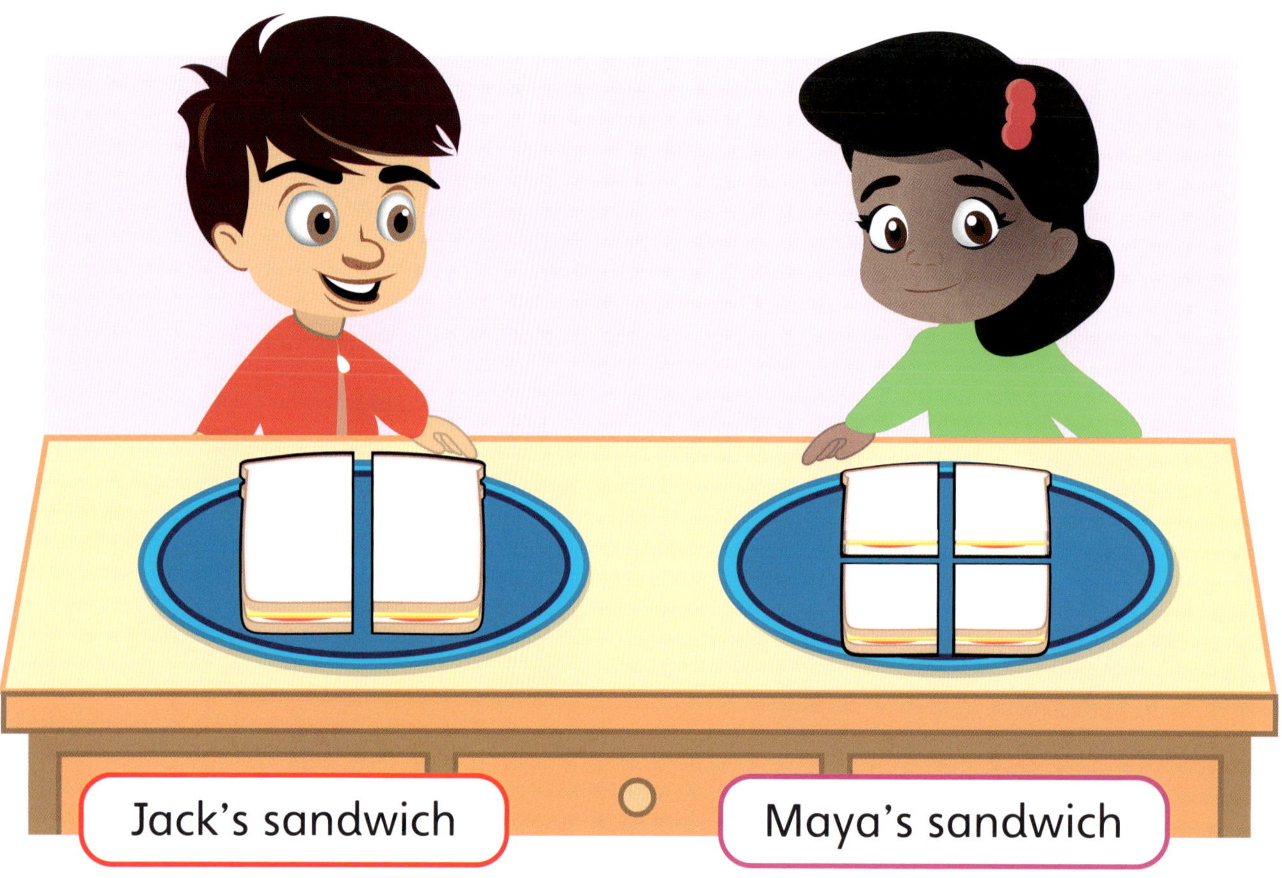

1 **a)** What fraction is Jack's sandwich cut into?

b) What is different about Maya's sandwich?

What is the same?

Share

a) Jack's sandwich is cut into halves.

He has two halves.

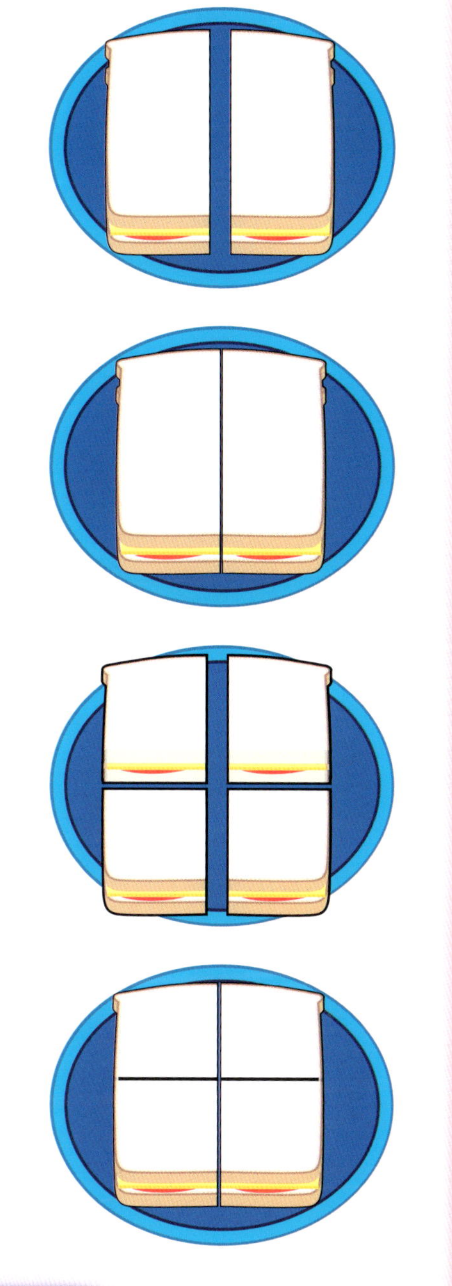

He has one whole sandwich.

Two halves equal one whole.

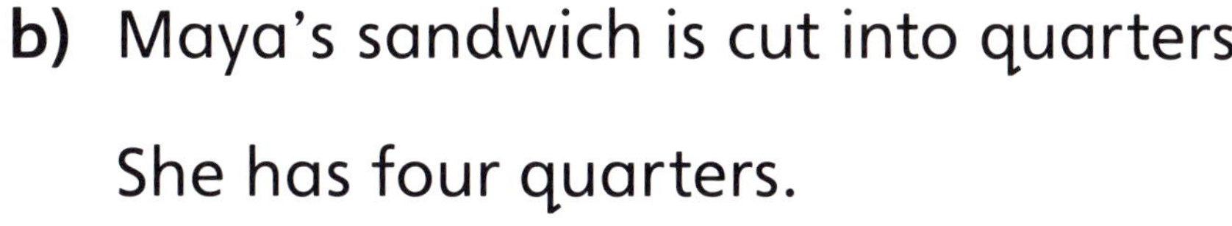

$\frac{2}{2} = 1$

b) Maya's sandwich is cut into quarters.

She has four quarters.

She has one whole sandwich.

Four quarters equal one whole.

$\frac{4}{4} = 1$

Think together

1 **a)** What fraction of each shape is shaded?

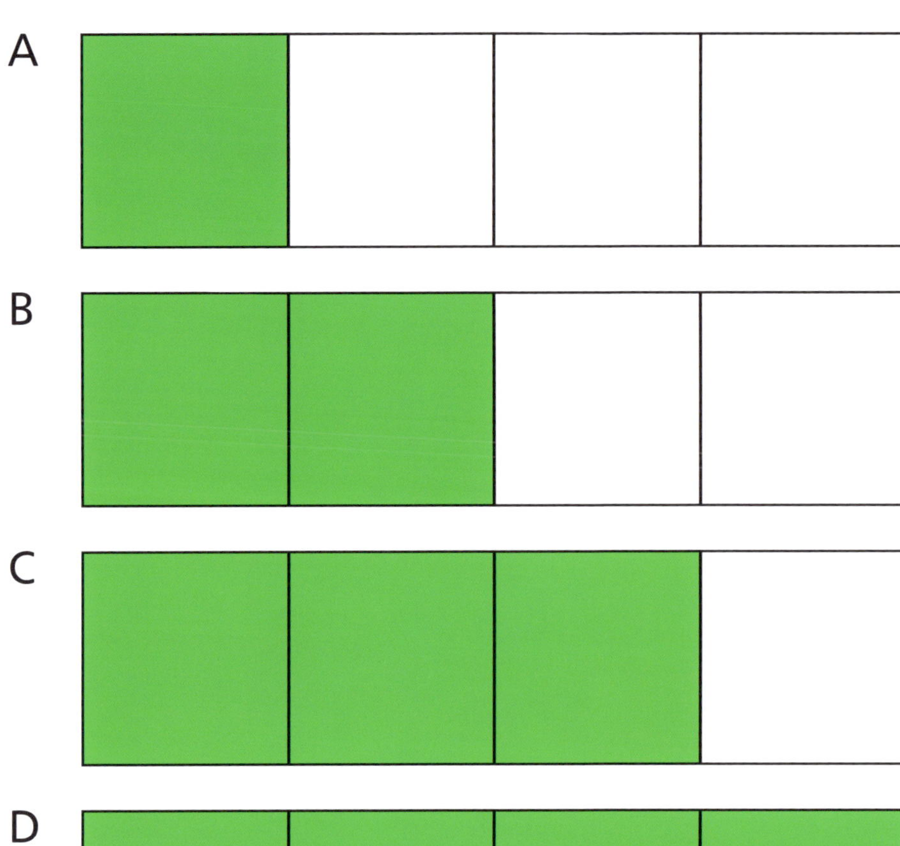

b) Which shape has the whole shaded?

2 Which fractions are equal to one whole?

$$\frac{3}{4} \qquad \frac{3}{3} \qquad \frac{2}{2} \qquad \frac{1}{2} \qquad \frac{4}{4}$$

3 Complete the number sentences.

a)

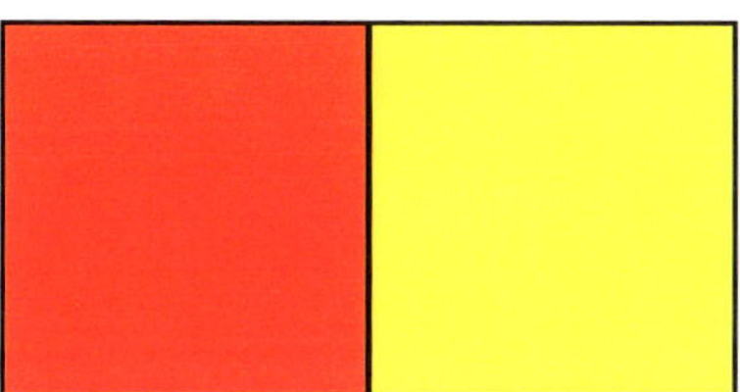

$$\frac{1}{2} + \frac{\boxed{}}{\boxed{}} = 1$$

b)

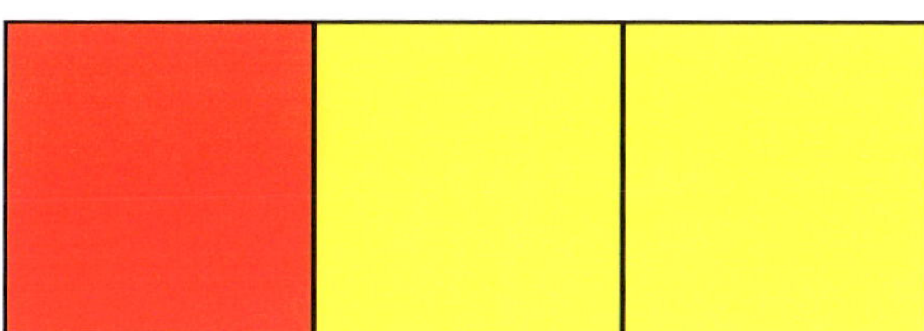

$$\frac{\boxed{}}{\boxed{}} + \frac{\boxed{}}{\boxed{}} = 1$$

c)

$$\frac{3}{4} + \frac{\boxed{}}{\boxed{}} = 1$$

→ Practice book 2C p39

End of unit check

1 Which shape has $\frac{1}{3}$ shaded?

A 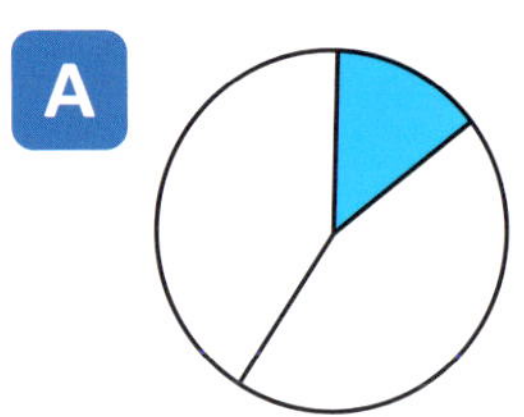 B C 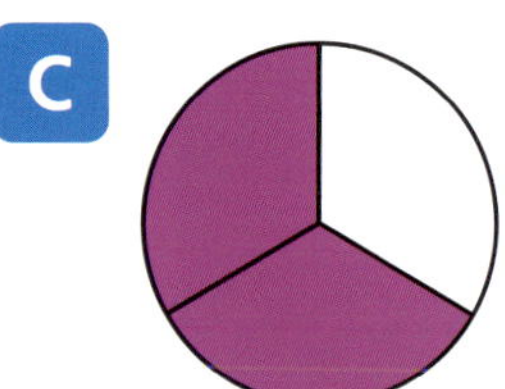 D 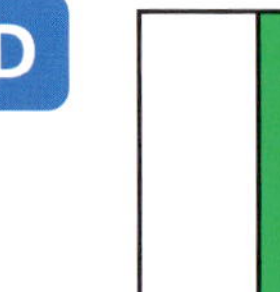

2 What is $\frac{1}{2}$ of 8?

A 16   B 5   C 4   D 3

3 Complete the number sentence. $\frac{\square}{\square}$ of 12 = 4.

A $\frac{1}{3}$ B $\frac{1}{4}$ C 16   D 8

4 What is the same as $\frac{1}{2}$ of 8?

A $\frac{1}{4}$ of 8   B $\frac{2}{4}$ of 8   C $\frac{1}{3}$ of 8   D $\frac{3}{4}$ of 8

5 Sara cuts a cake into 4 equal pieces.

She eats 3 pieces. How much has she eaten?

A $\frac{1}{4}$ B $\frac{2}{4}$ C $\frac{3}{4}$ D $\frac{4}{4}$

Think!

Here are eight fractions.

$\frac{1}{4}$ $\frac{1}{2}$ $\frac{1}{3}$ $\frac{2}{4}$ $\frac{3}{4}$ $\frac{2}{2}$ $\frac{4}{4}$ $\frac{3}{3}$

Sort the fractions into groups.

Explain how you have sorted them.

unit fraction   non-unit fraction

quarters   thirds

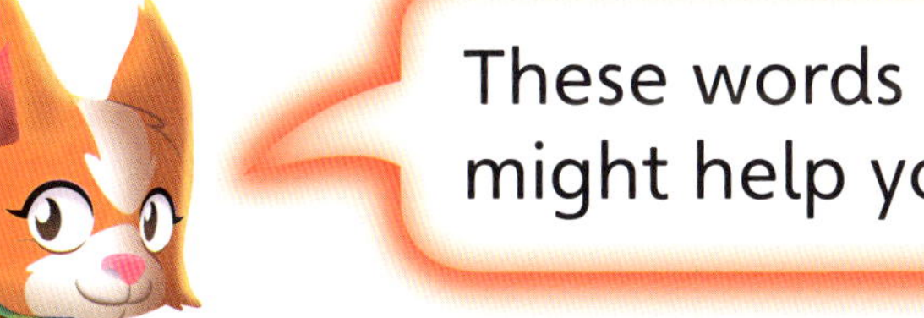

halves   half

whole   part

→ Practice book 2C p42

Unit 11
Time

In this unit we will …
- ⚡ Tell time to the hour and half hour
- ⚡ Tell the time to quarter to and quarter past
- ⚡ Tell the time to 5 minutes
- ⚡ Learn about minutes and hours

Do you remember which is the hour hand and which is the minute hand?

o'clock

half past

quarter past

quarter to

minute hand

hour hand

hours

minutes

O'clock and half past

Discover

1 **a)** What times do the trips leave?

b) What time do you think the last clock will show?

Share

a)

o'clock

half past

When the minute hand points to 12 it is an **o'clock** time. When it points to 6 it is a half-past time.

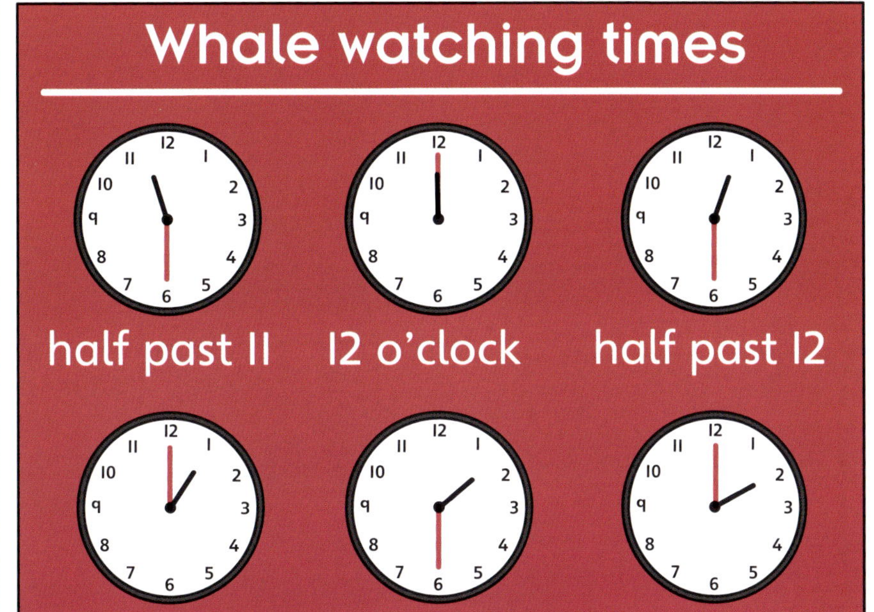

b) The next half-past time after 2 o'clock looks like this.

The last clock will show half past 2.

Think together

1 What time is it?

a)

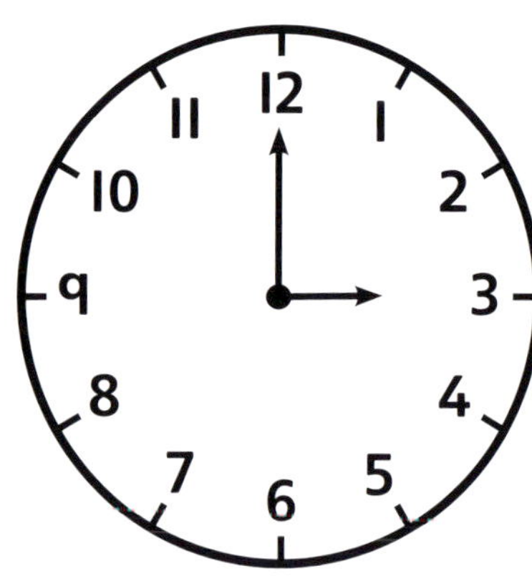

b)

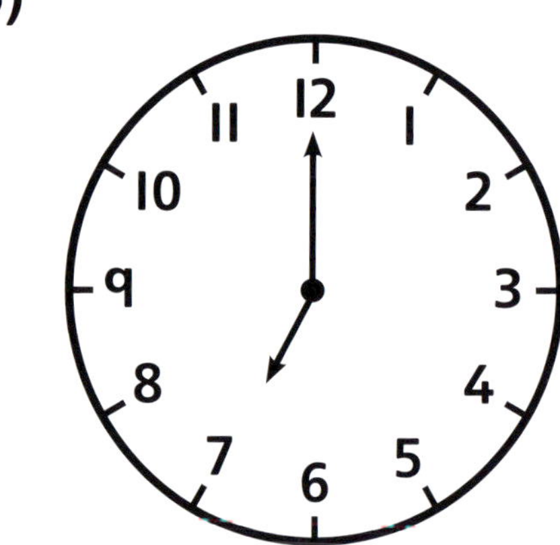

2 What time is it?

a)

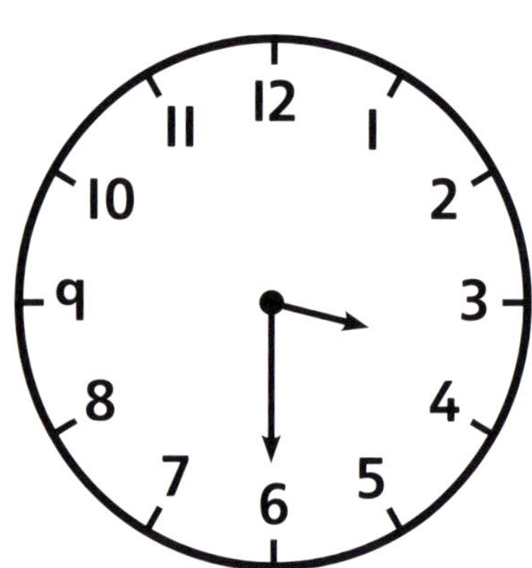

b)

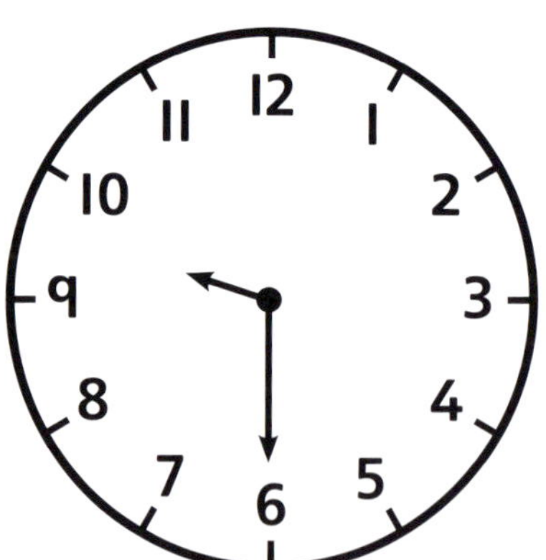

3 **a)** Which circle would you sort each clock into?

CHALLENGE

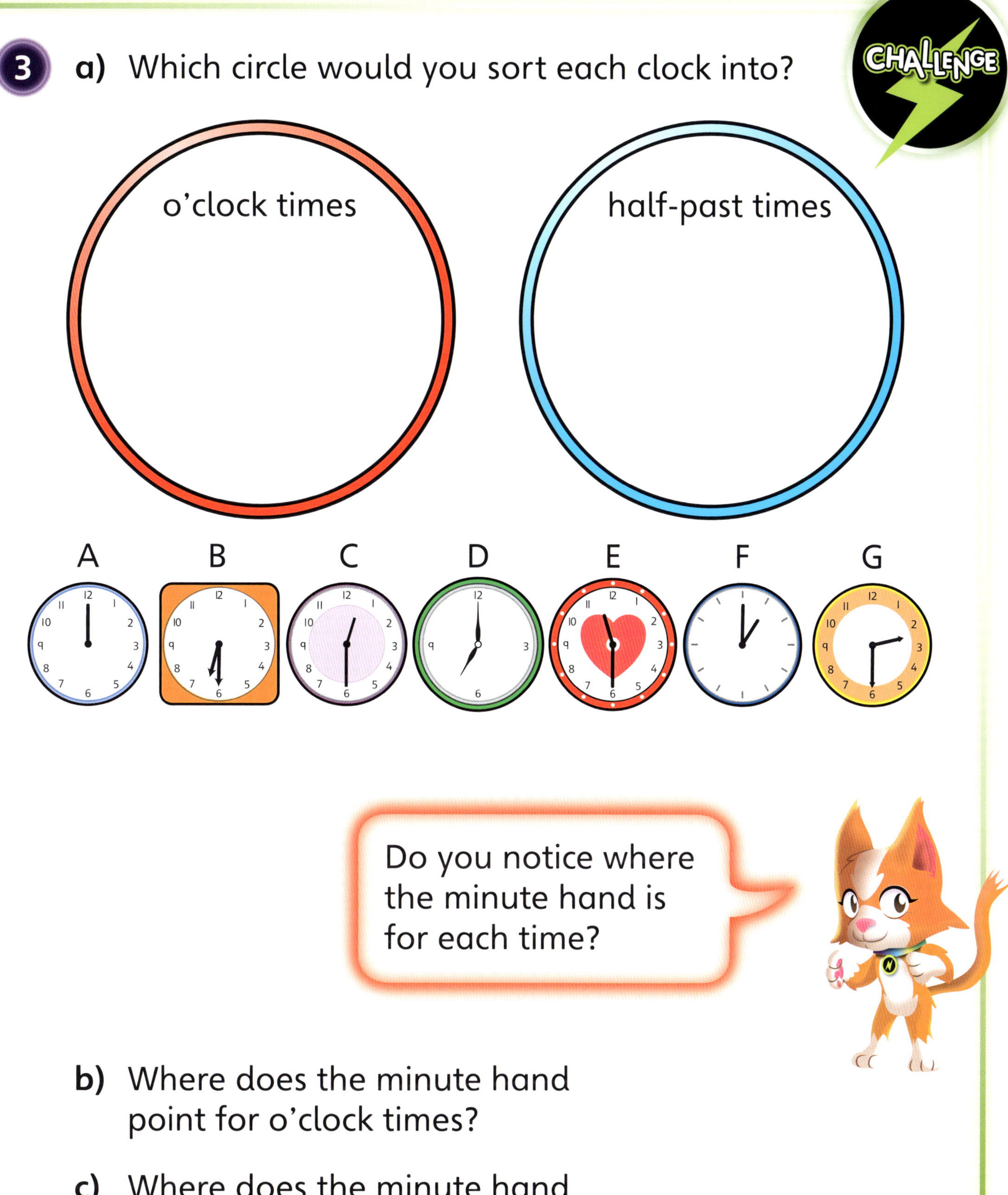

b) Where does the minute hand
point for o'clock times?

c) Where does the minute hand
point for half-past times?

63

→ **Practice book 2C p44**

Quarter past and quarter to

Discover

1 **a)** What time will the tiger be fed?

b) What time will the penguin be fed?

Share

a)

o'clock	quarter past	half past	quarter to

The tiger will be fed at quarter past 5.

b) The penguin will be fed at quarter to 6.

Think together

1 a) What time does the reptile house open?

b) What time does it close?

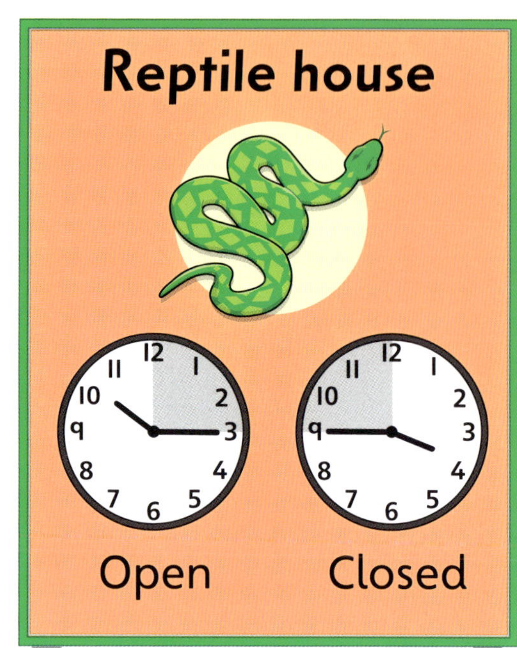

2 What times can you meet the macaws?

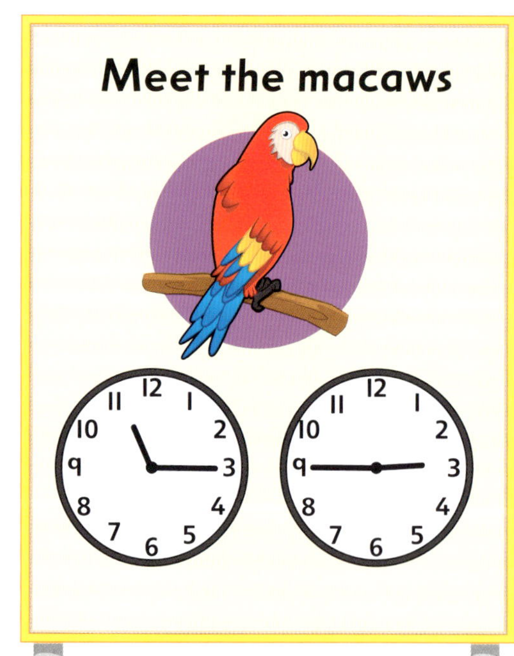

3

CHALLENGE

Anna

Kat

Milo

Kat is going to make quarter past 5.

Milo is going to make quarter to 1.

Make or draw your own quarter-past and quarter-to times.

Can you read a partner's times?

→ Practice book 2C p47

Tell the time to 5 minutes

Discover

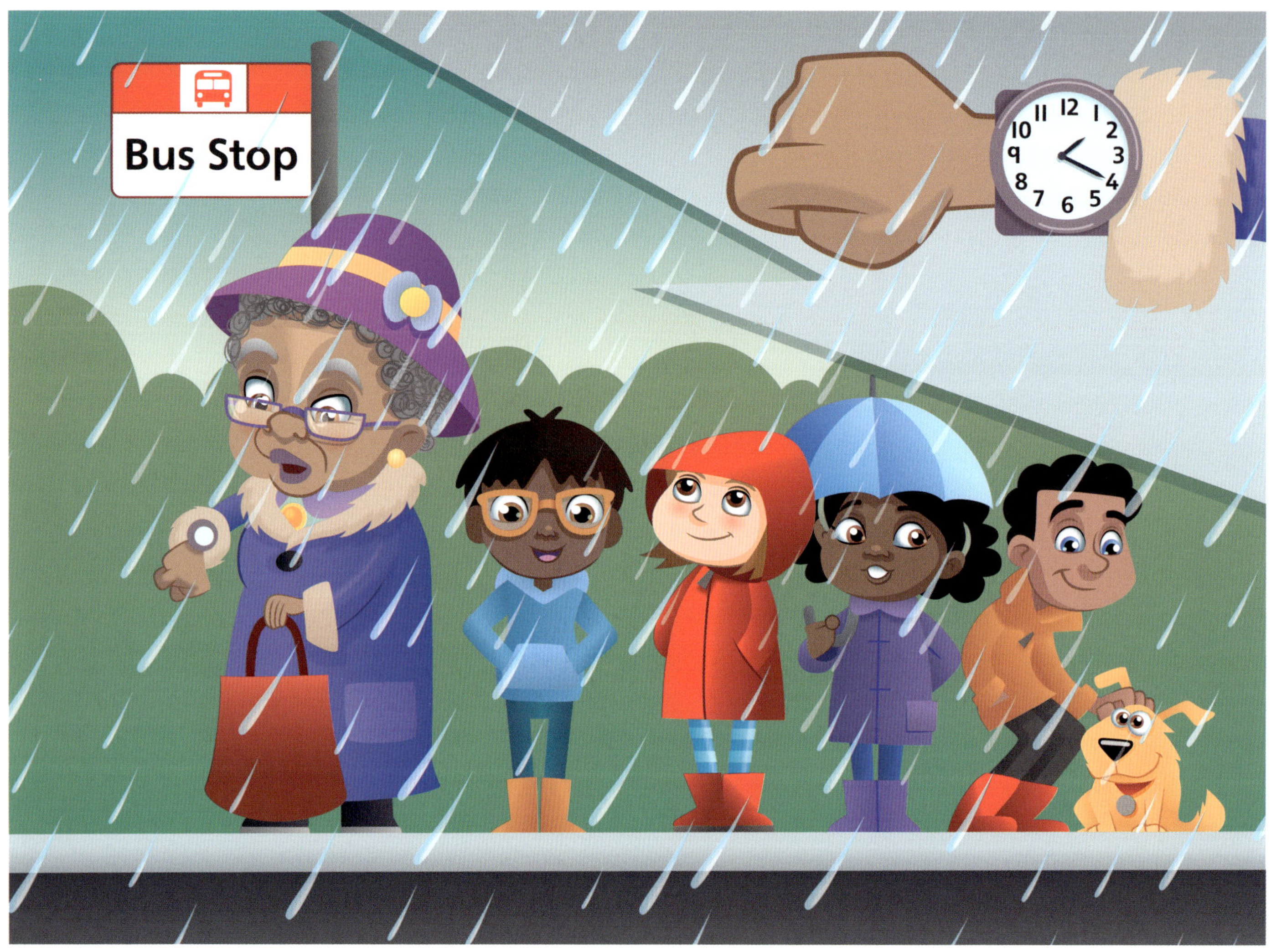

1 **a)** The bus is due to arrive in 5 minutes.

What time will the bus arrive?

b) What time will the bus arrive if it is 15 minutes late?

Share

a)

> Each number on the clock represents another 5 minutes, so you can count in 5s.

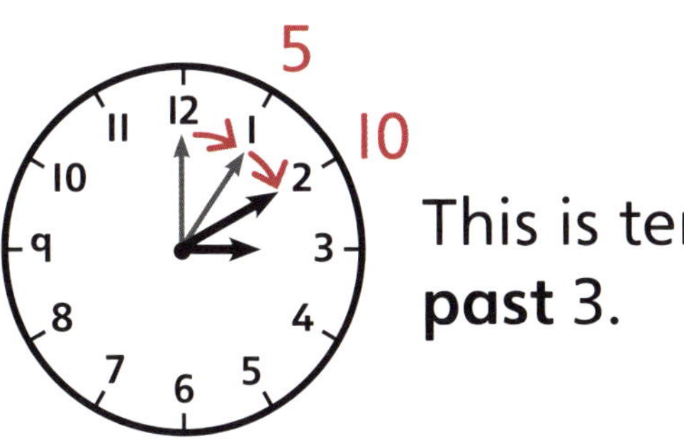

This is ten **past** 3.

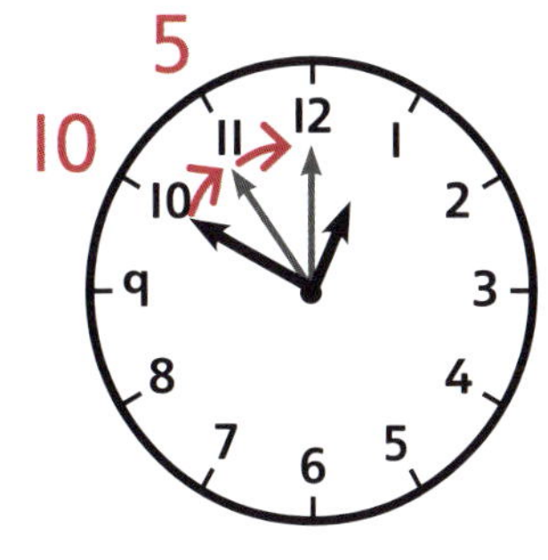

This is ten **to** 1.

Count in 5s to find the answer.

The time now is 20 minutes past 1.

In another 5 minutes the time will be:

The bus will arrive at **25 minutes past 1**.

b) The bus was due at 25 minutes past 1.

Count on 15 minutes.   Then work out the new time.

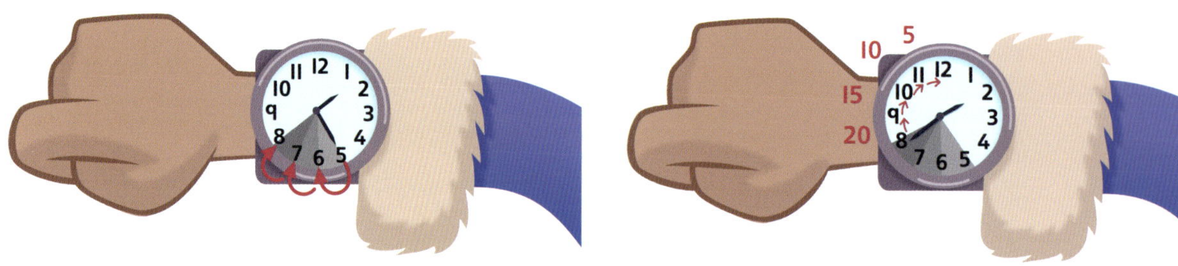

The bus will arrive at 20 minutes to 2.

Think together

1 What time is it?

a)

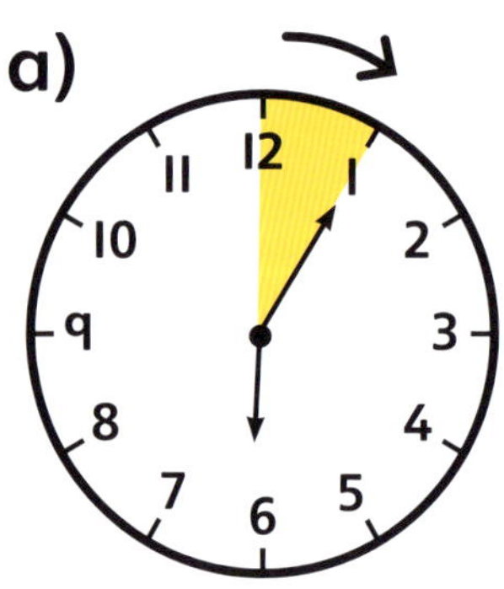

c)

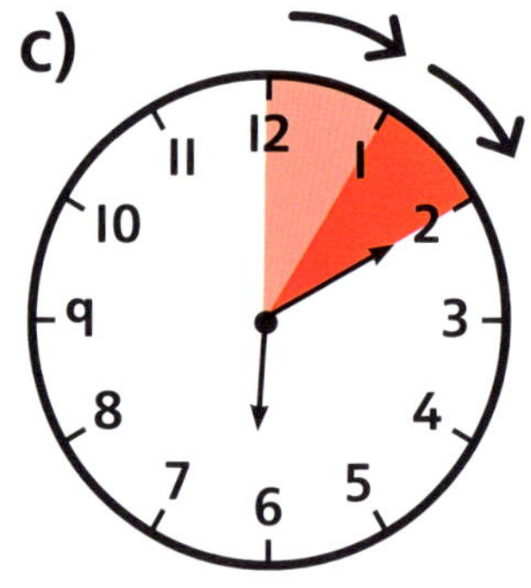

b)

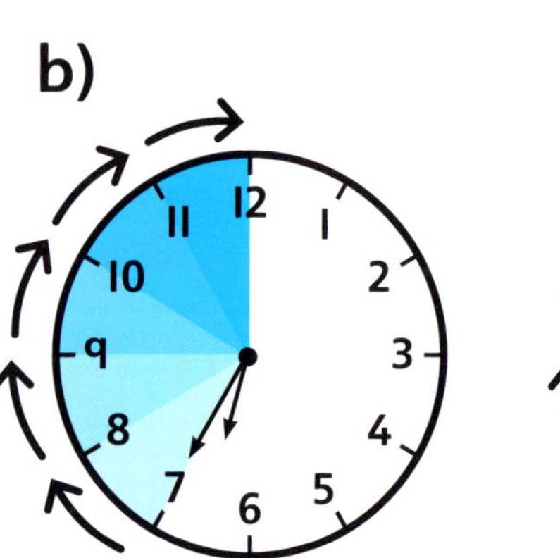

d)

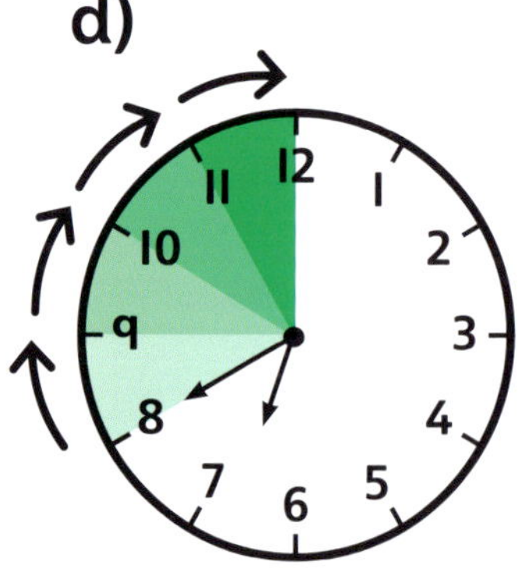

2 What time is it?

a)

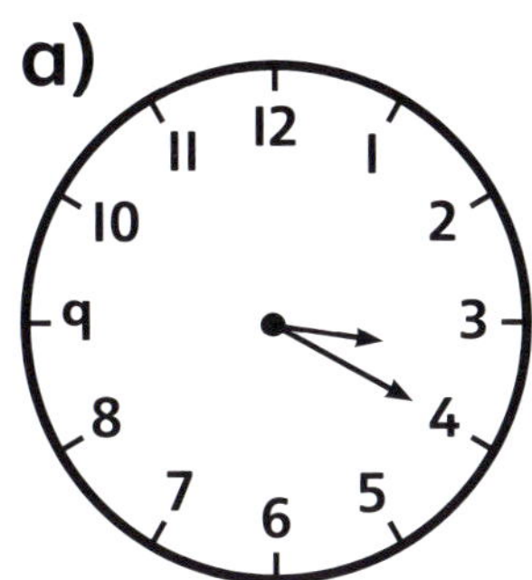

b)

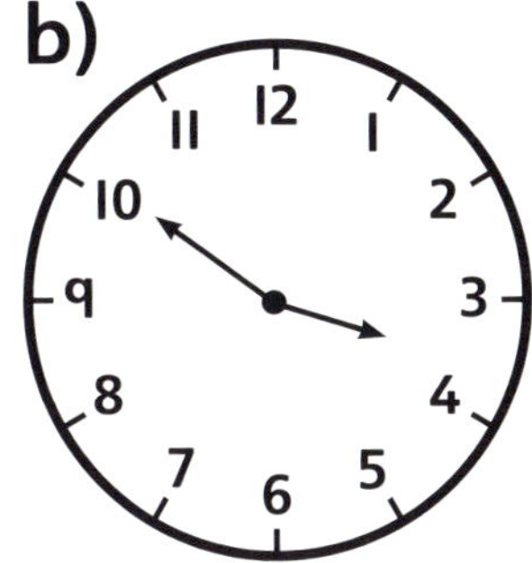

c)

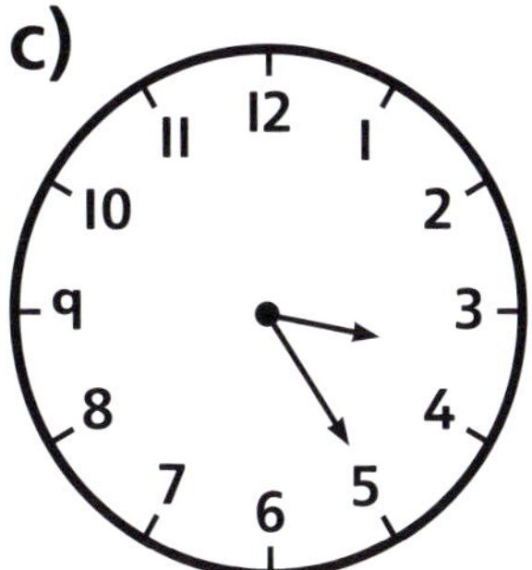

d)

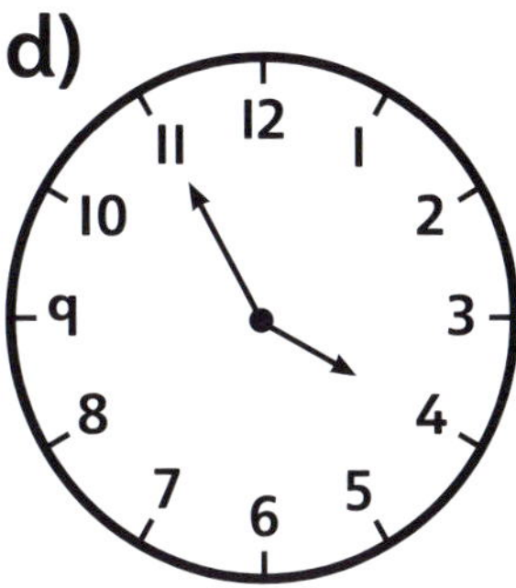

3 How many clock times can you show between 8 o'clock and 9 o'clock?

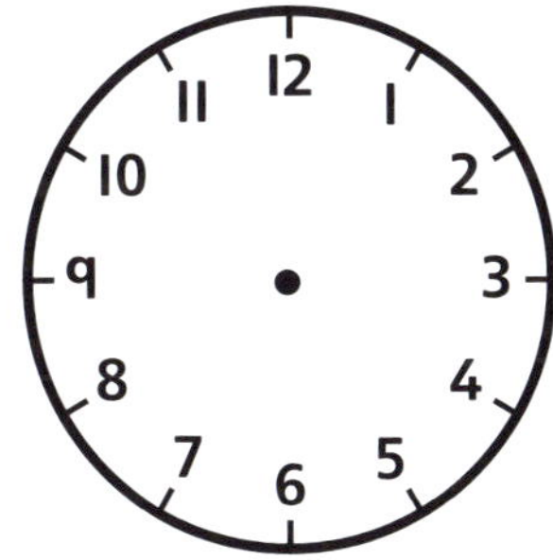

71

Minutes in an hour

Discover

1 **a)** Joe took 80 minutes to run the race.

How many hours and minutes did he take?

b) Who took longer out of Eve and Anya?

Share

a)

There are 60 minutes in 1 hour.

I used this to help me find the time Joe took in hours and minutes.

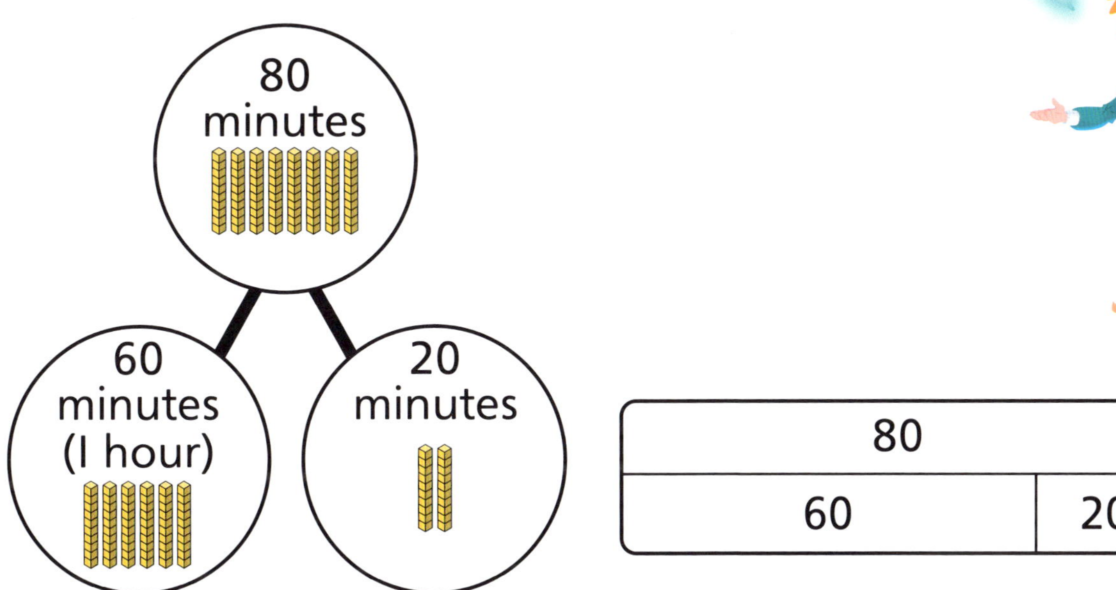

80 minutes is the same as 1 hour and 20 minutes.

Joe took 1 hour and 20 minutes.

b) Anya took 55 minutes. Eve took 1 hour 10 minutes.

It is easier to compare measurements if they both have the same units.

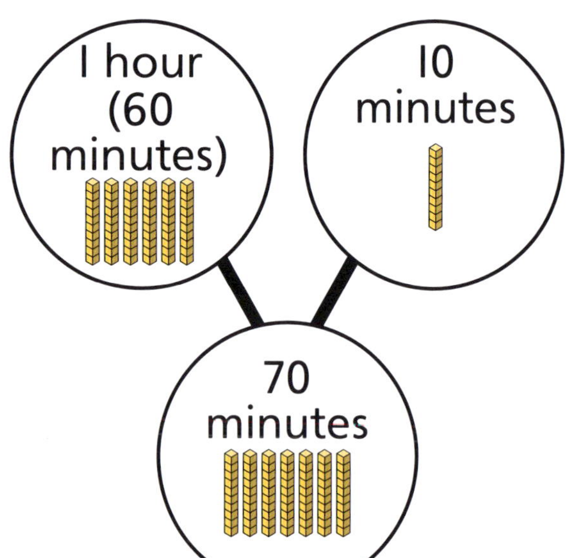

1 hour and 10 minutes is the same as 70 minutes.

Anya took 55 minutes.
Eve took 70 minutes.

Eve took longer.

Think together

 **a)**

1 hour is the same as ⬚ minutes.

b)

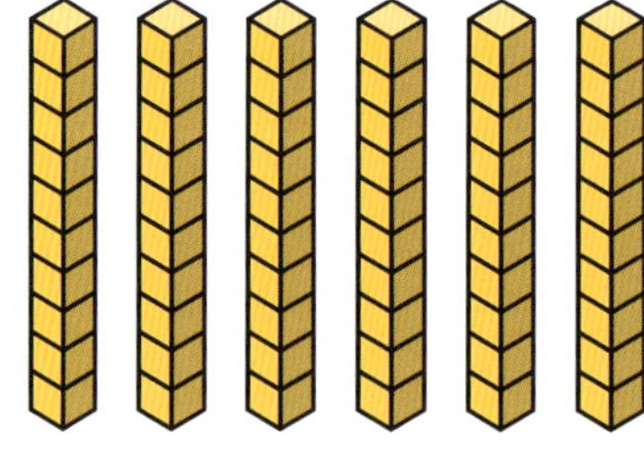

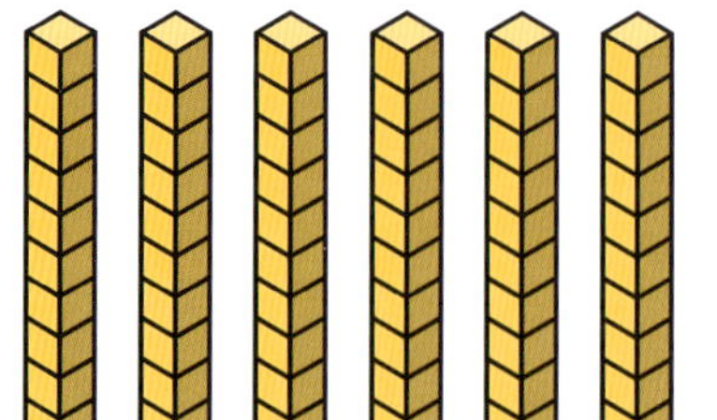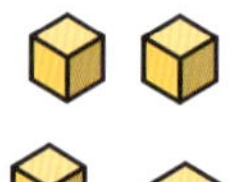

 1 hour and 5 minutes is the same as ⬚ minutes.

2

[ ] hour and [ ] minutes is the same as [ ] minutes.

3 What is 95 minutes written in hours and minutes?

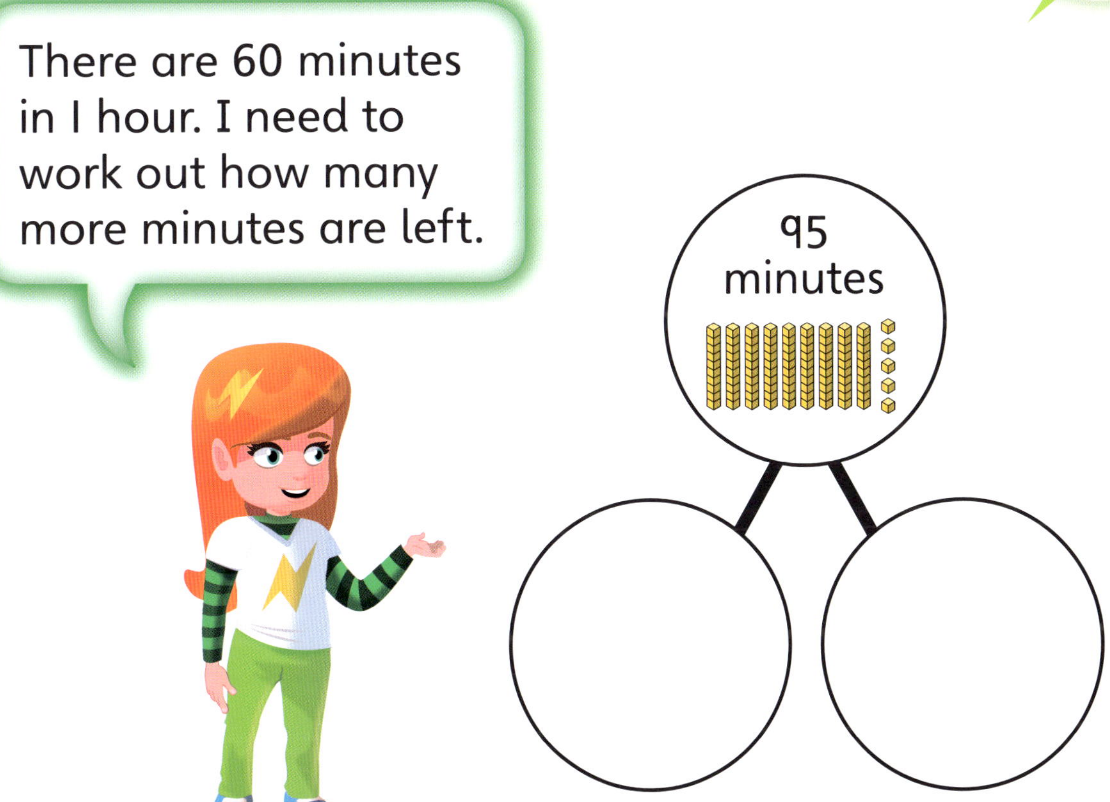

→ Practice book 2C p53

Hours in a day

Discover

1 a) How many times in a day does the hour hand go around the clock?

How many hours are there in one day?

b) Should Sunil drink the smoothie? Why?

Share

a)

There are **24** hours in one day.

b) Look at the time Sunil wants to drink the smoothie.

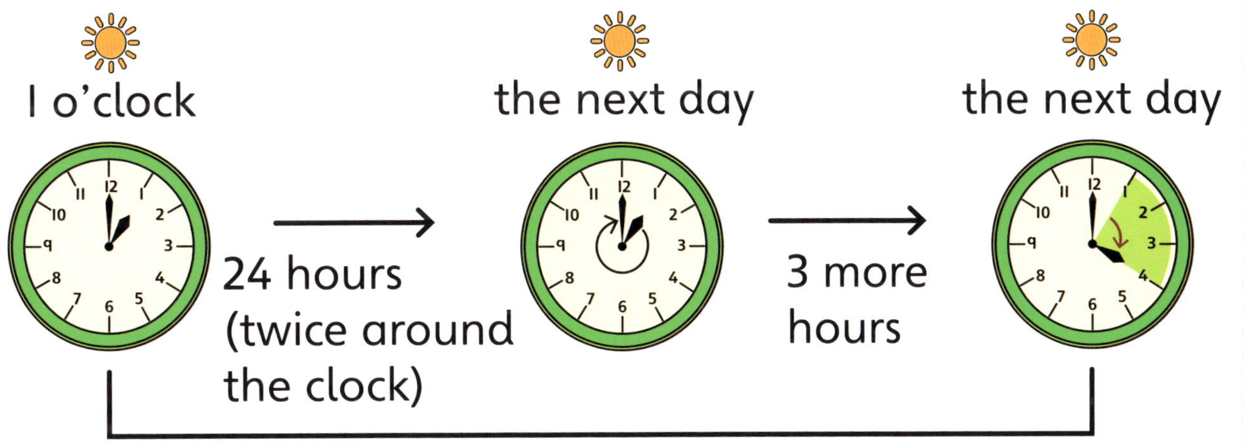

4 o'clock is **more than** 24 hours later.

Sunil should not drink the smoothie as it is not safe to drink.

It should have been drunk by 1 o'clock in the daytime the next day.

Think together

1 Today is Tuesday. When will the postal worker be back?

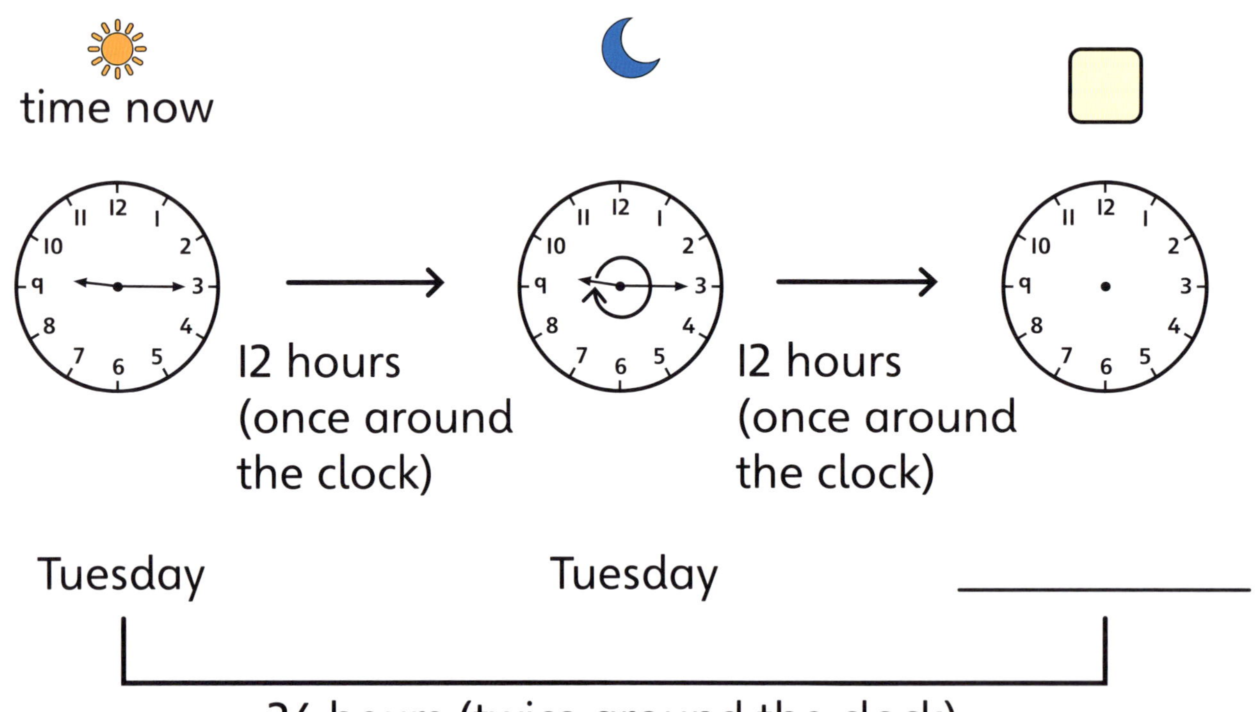

2

When can the bandage be taken off?

3 An explorer wants to climb a mountain in 24 hours.

Here are the times when she started and finished her climb.

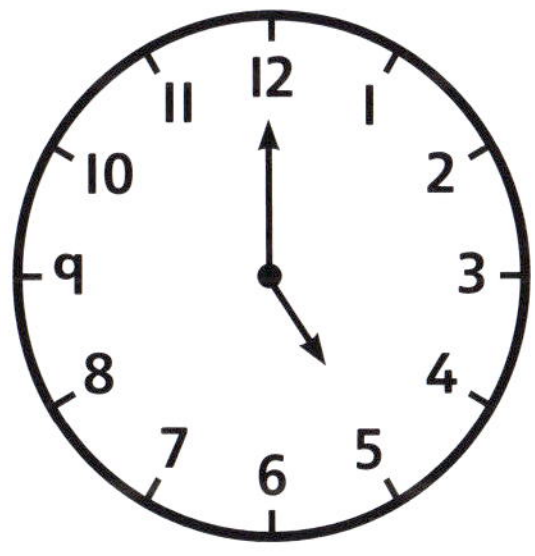

start time

end time

a) Did she climb the mountain in time?

b) What else do you need to know to answer the question?

→ **Practice book 2C p56**

End of unit check

1 What time does the clock show?

A 5 o'clock

C 6 o'clock

B half past 5

D 25 past 6

2 What time is shown?

A quarter past 9

C quarter past 10

B quarter to 11

D 10 minutes to 3

3 PE is at 5 minutes to 2. What will the clock look like?

A  **B**   **C** **D** 

4 Children were timed solving a maze.

Alex	Olivia	Ella
1 hour and 20 minutes	85 minutes	1 hour and 30 minutes

Who left the maze first?

A Alex

C Ella

B Olivia

D Olivia and Ella left together

5 A car is parked on Thursday morning at this time.
It can stay for 24 hours. When does it have to move? 

A On Friday at 10 minutes to 11 in the night.

B On Thursday at 10 minutes to 11 in the night.

C On Friday at 10 minutes past 11 in the day.

D On Friday at 10 minutes to 11 in the day.

Think!

These times have been given for you.

Explain how you know they are right.

25 minutes past 6

20 minutes to 3

hour hand

minute hand

→ Practice book 2C p59

Unit 12
Problem solving and efficient methods

In this unit we will …
- ⚡ Compare ways of calculating
- ⚡ Use mental addition and subtraction
- ⚡ Look for the most efficient way to solve a problem
- ⚡ Use number facts to solve problems
- ⚡ Solve word problems using all four operations

1	2	3	4	5	6	7	8	9	10
11	12	13	14	15	16	17	18	19	20
21	22	23	24	25	26	27	28	29	30
31	32	33	34	35	36	37	38	39	40
41	42	43	44	45	46	47	48	49	50
51	52	53	54	55	56	57	58	59	60
61	62	63	64	65	66	67	68	69	70
71	72	73	74	75	76	77	78	79	80
81	82	83	84	85	86	87	88	89	90
91	92	93	94	95	96	97	98	99	100

We will need some maths words.
Have you heard any of these before?

number facts

calculate mentally

bar model

partition

number line

part-whole model

100 square

We can use a bar model to help
us add, subtract, multiply and
divide. Can you use this bar model
to calculate 17 + ☐ = 40?

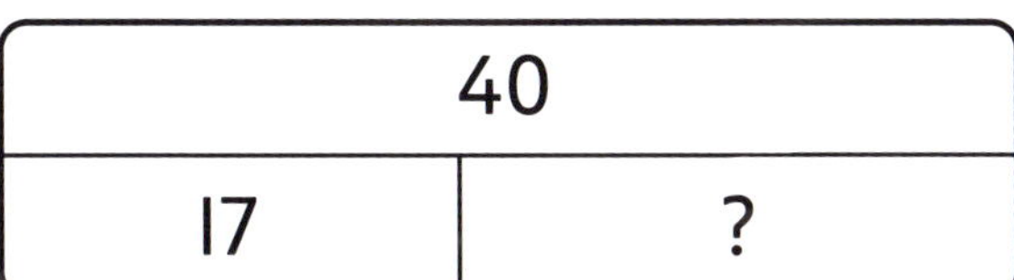

40	
17	?

My way, your way!

Discover

1 **a)** How much does it cost to post the parcel?

b) How much does it cost to post the parcel and the letter?

Share

a) The letter costs 35p.

The parcel costs 15p more than the letter.

The parcel costs 50p to post.

b)

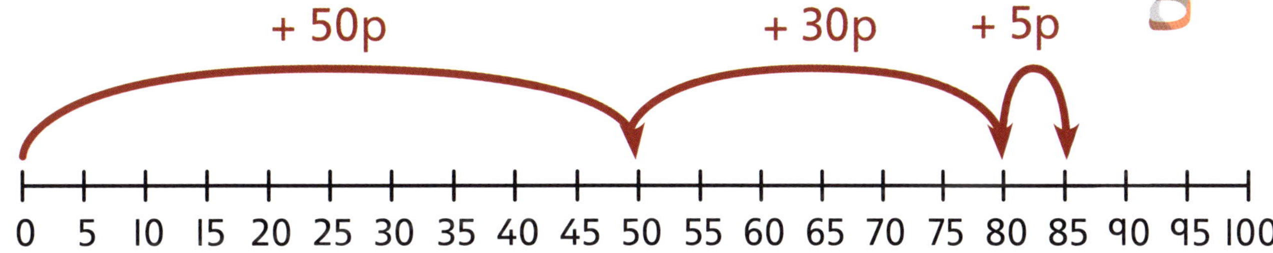

The cost of posting the letter and the parcel is 85p.

Think together

1 Sam wants to post 2 cards using next-day delivery.

He has £1.

Does he have enough money?

Price list for posting a card	
Normal delivery	35p
Next-day delivery	45p
Signed for	Extra 20p

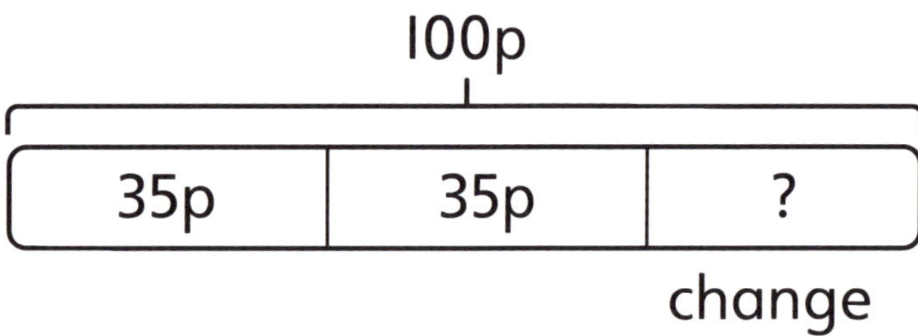

2 Sam sends 2 cards using normal delivery.

How much change will he get from £1?

change

3

Seth has £1. Is that enough money?

Card 1

Card 2

→ **Practice book 2C p61**

Use number facts

Discover

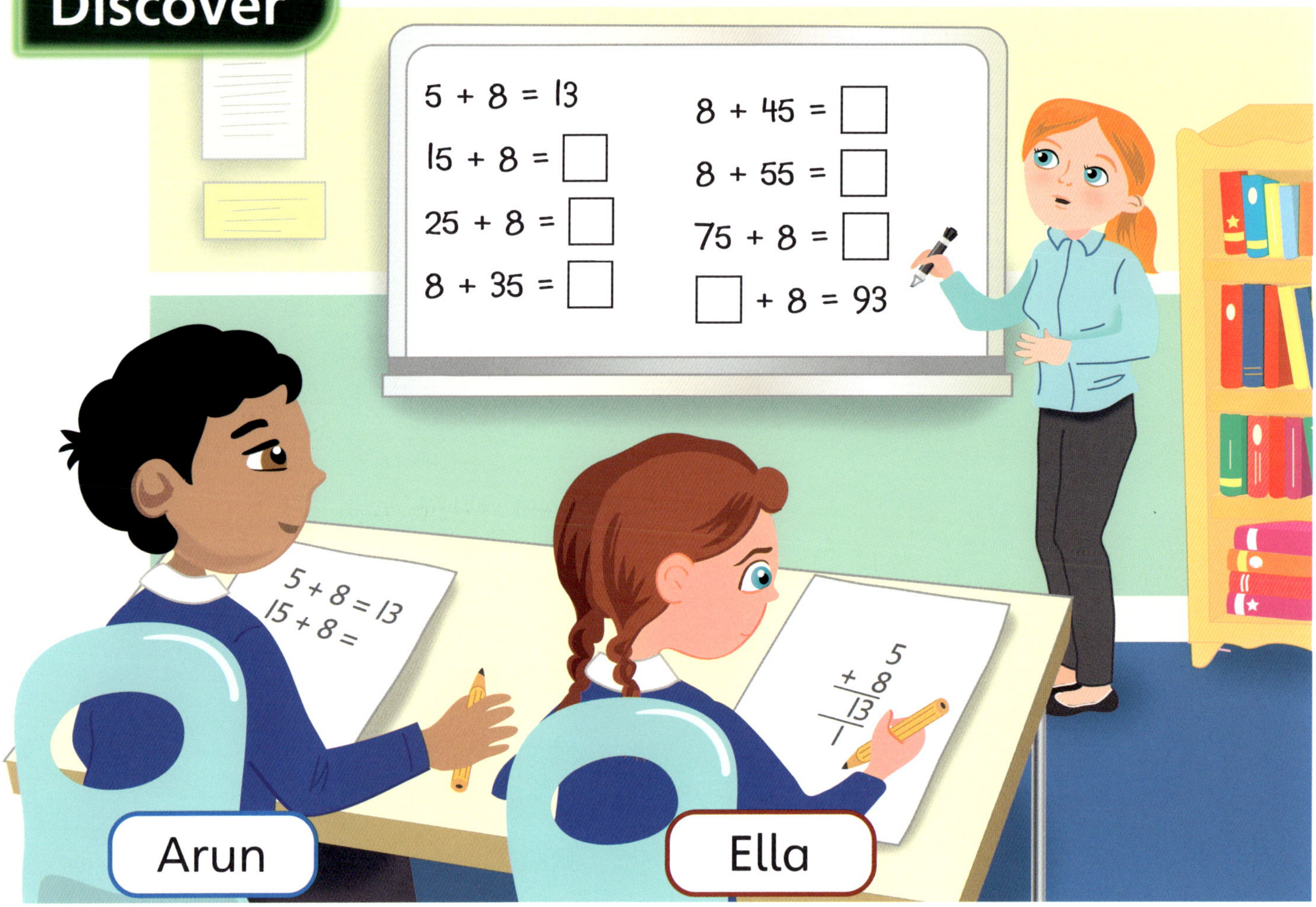

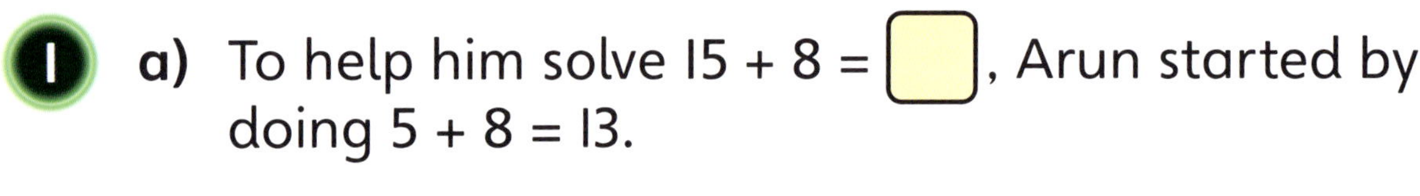

1 a) To help him solve $15 + 8 = \boxed{}$, Arun started by doing $5 + 8 = 13$.

Explain his strategy.

b) Use the same strategy to solve these:

$25 + 8 = \boxed{}$

$35 + 8 = \boxed{}$

Share

a)

5 + 8 = 13

15 is 10 more than 5.

15 + 8 must be 10 more than 5 + 8.

15 + 8 = 23

Arun added the 1s first, then added the 10.

b) 25 + 8

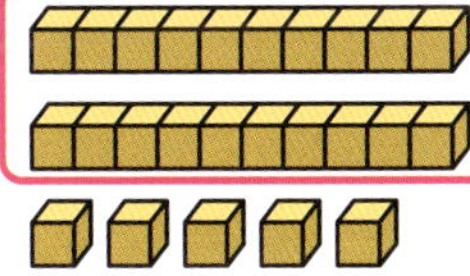
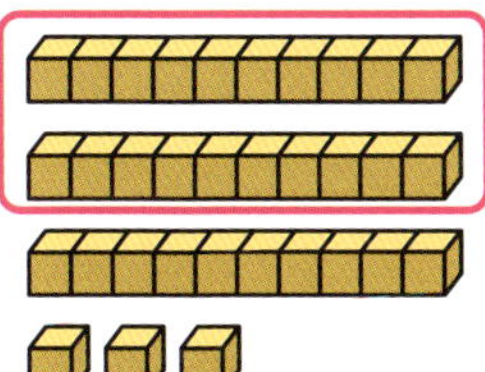

25 + 8 = 33

35 + 8

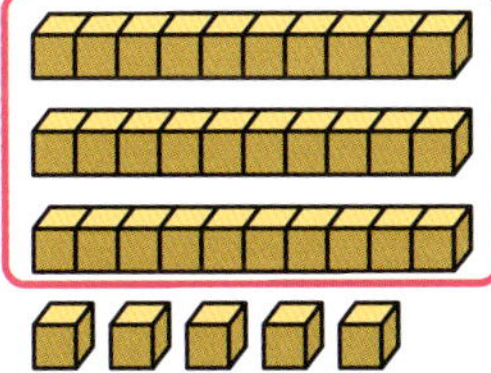
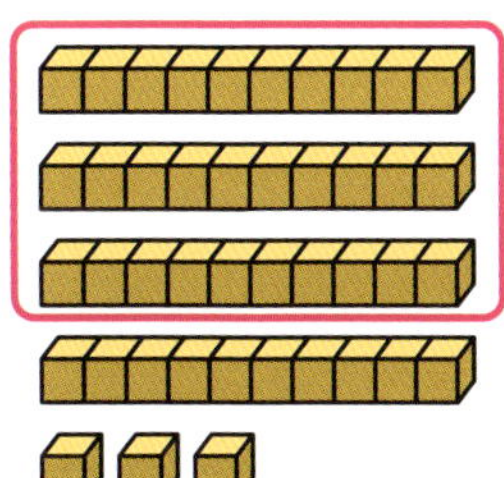

35 + 8 = 43

89

Think together

 1

$$59 + 6 = 65$$

Use this calculation to work out:

a) 79 + 6

79 is ☐ more than 59.

Therefore 79 + 6 = ☐.

b) 29 + 6

29 is ☐ less than 59.

Therefore 29 + 6 = ☐.

2

$$24 + 37 = 61$$

Use this calculation to work out 24 + 67.

3

$$28 + 36 = \boxed{}$$

Work out the answer.

How could you use it to help these children work out their answers?

→ Practice book 2C p64

Use a 100 square

Discover

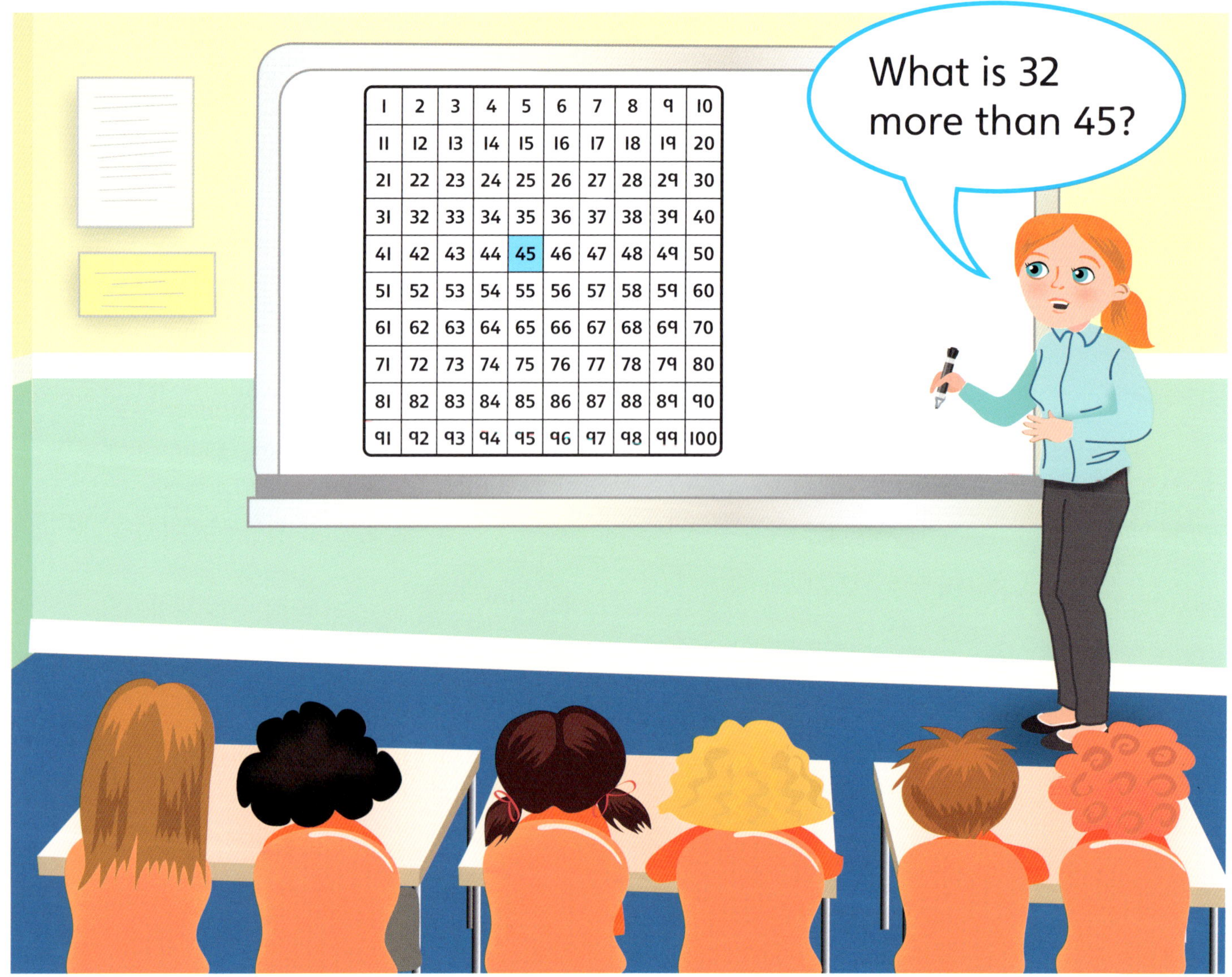

1 **a)** What is 8 more than 45?
How can you use the 100 square for support?

b) What is 32 more than 45?
How can you use the 100 square for support?

Share

a)

Count on 8 from 45.

46, 47, 48, 49, 50, 51, 52, 53

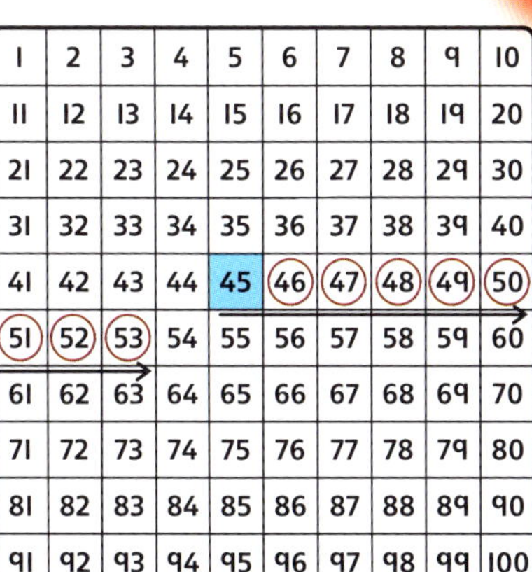

Or count on 10 by moving down to the next row. Then count back 2, because 10 is 2 more than 8.

45, 55, 54, 53

So, the answer is 45 + 8 = 53.

b) Count on in 10s from 45. Then count on in 1s from 75.

55, 65, 75, 76, 77

So the answer is 45 + 32 = 77.

Think together

1 What is 36 more than 52?

1	2	3	4	5	6	7	8	9	10
11	12	13	14	15	16	17	18	19	20
21	22	23	24	25	26	27	28	29	30
31	32	33	34	35	36	37	38	39	40
41	42	43	44	45	46	47	48	49	50
51	52	53	54	55	56	57	58	59	60
61	62	63	64	65	66	67	68	69	70
71	72	73	74	75	76	77	78	79	80
81	82	83	84	85	86	87	88	89	90
91	92	93	94	95	96	97	98	99	100

2 What is 45 less than 76?

1	2	3	4	5	6	7	8	9	10
11	12	13	14	15	16	17	18	19	20
21	22	23	24	25	26	27	28	29	30
31	32	33	34	35	36	37	38	39	40
41	42	43	44	45	46	47	48	49	50
51	52	53	54	55	56	57	58	59	60
61	62	63	64	65	66	67	68	69	70
71	72	73	74	75	76	77	78	79	80
81	82	83	84	85	86	87	88	89	90
91	92	93	94	95	96	97	98	99	100

3 Millie is working out 68 − 26 on a 100 square.

1	2	3	4	5	6	7	8	9	10
11	12	13	14	15	16	17	18	19	20
21	22	23	24	25	26	27	28	29	30
31	32	33	34	35	36	37	38	39	40
41	42	43	44	45	46	47	48	49	50
51	52	53	54	55	56	57	58	59	60
61	62	63	64	65	66	67	68	69	70
71	72	73	74	75	76	77	78	79	80
81	82	83	84	85	86	87	88	89	90
91	92	93	94	95	96	97	98	99	100

Show Millie's calculation on a number line.

→ **Practice book 2C p67**

Getting started

Discover

1 **a)** Each child has a set of number cards from 1 to 9. Which two cards could Filip have?

☐ + ☐ = 14

b) One of Kat's numbers is the same as Filip's. Which three cards could Kat have?

☐ + ☐ + ☐ = 14

Share

a)

2   If Filip picks up 2: $14 - 2 = 12$

There is no card for 12, the biggest number is 9.

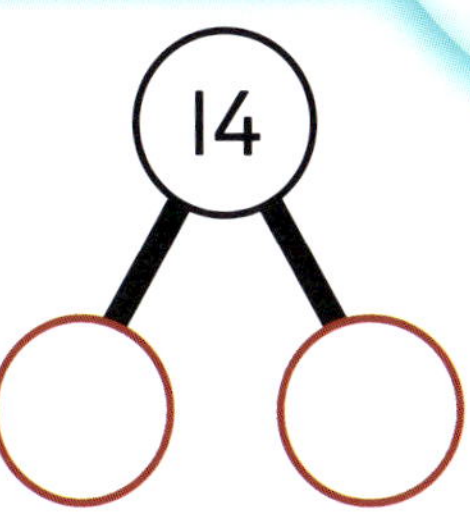

9   If Filip picks up 9: $14 - 9 = 5$

There is a card for 5.

$9 + 5 = 14$

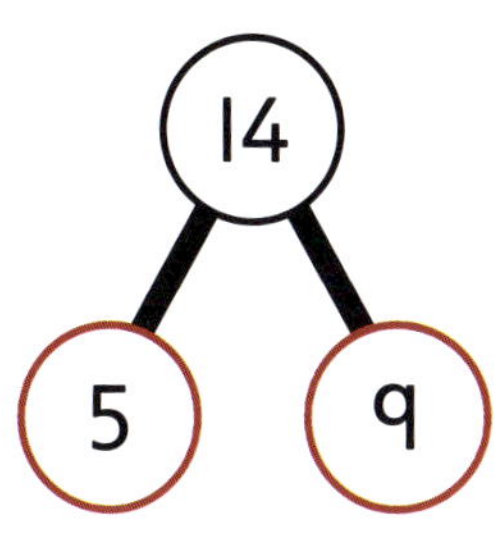

Filip could have the cards 9 and 5. Or he could have the cards 8 and 6.

b) $9 + 5 = 14$

Partition 9 or 5 to find three numbers which total 14.

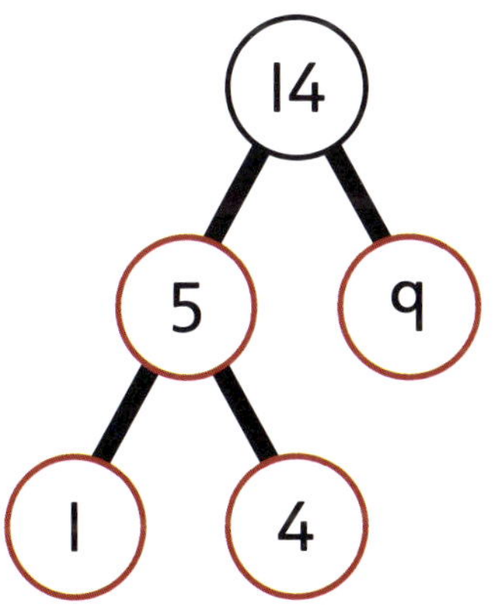

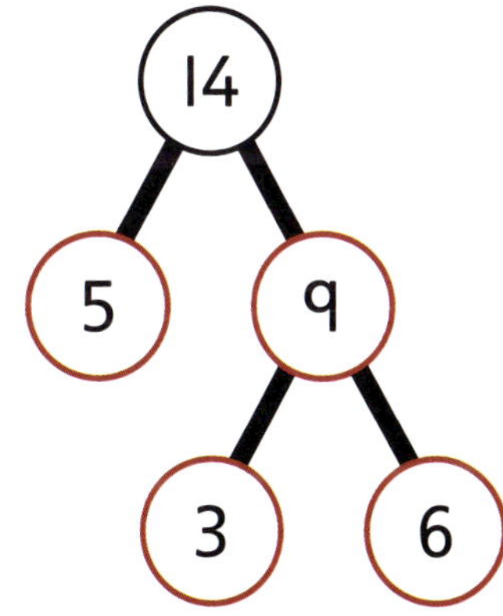

$1 + 4 + 9 = 14$ $5 + 3 + 6 = 14$

Kat could have the cards 1, 9 and 4. Or she could have the cards 5, 3 and 6.

Think together

1 Find all the pairs of cards that add up to 14.

Use a part-whole model to help you.

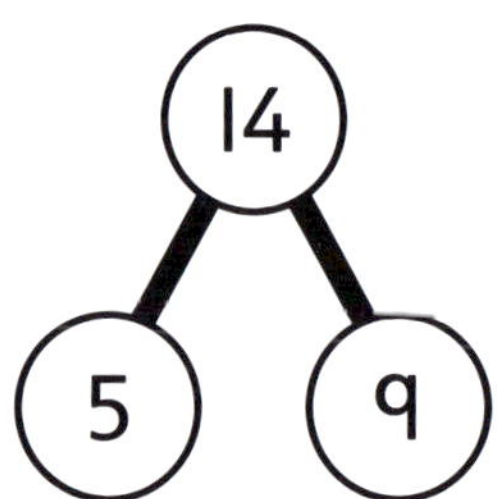

First card	1	2	3	4	5	6	7	8	9
Second card	13	12			9				

2 Find two more sets of three numbers which add up to 14.

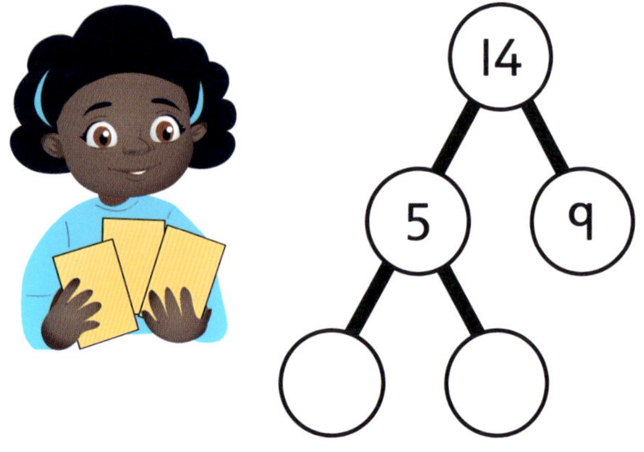

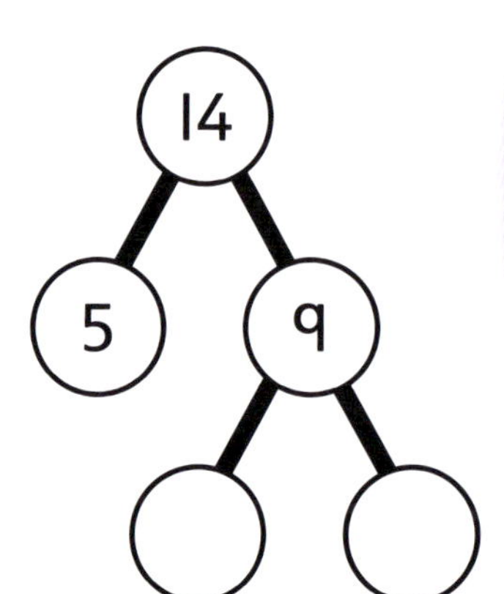

3 Both children make 14 using only one set of number cards, 1 to 9, shared between them.

| 1 | 2 | 3 | 4 | 5 | 6 | 7 | 8 | 9 |

What could their numbers be?

Use what you found out in question 1 to help you.

→ **Practice book 2C p70**

Missing numbers

Discover

1 **a)** How much money did Marta have before her father gave her £20?

b) Marta wants to donate £100 to a charity that protects birds. How much more does she need to save?

Share

a)

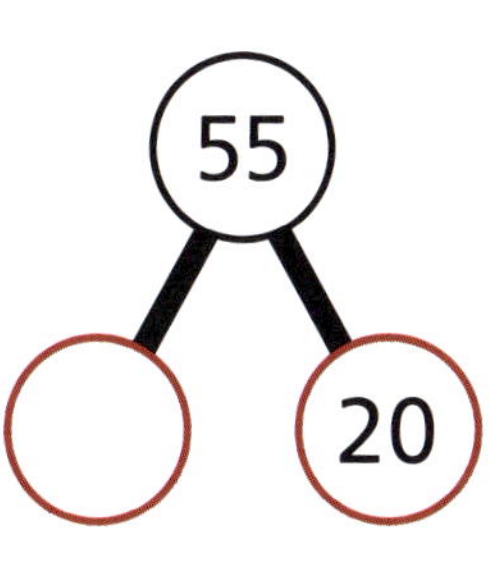

55

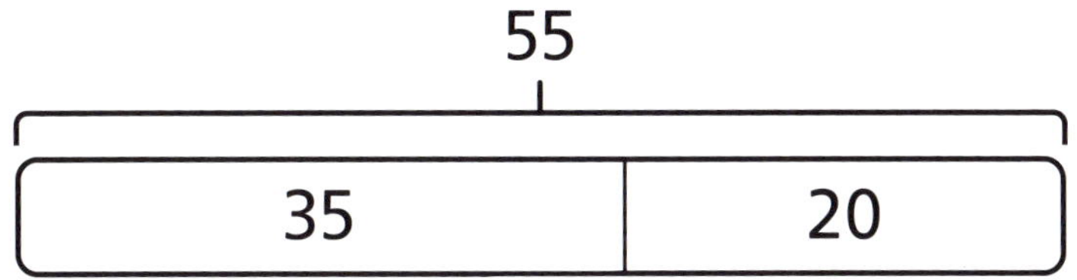

| 35 | 20 |

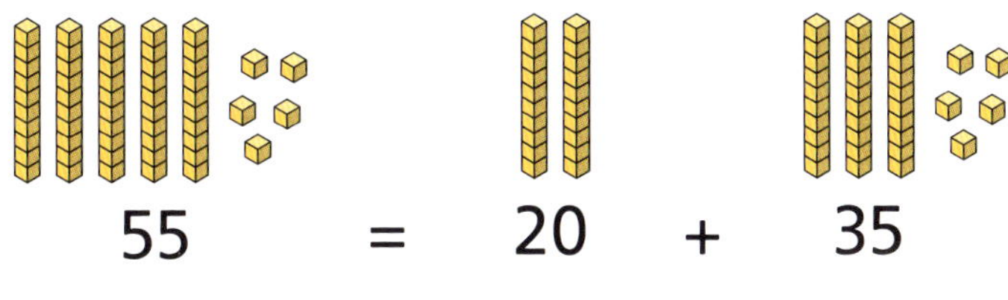

55 = 20 + 35

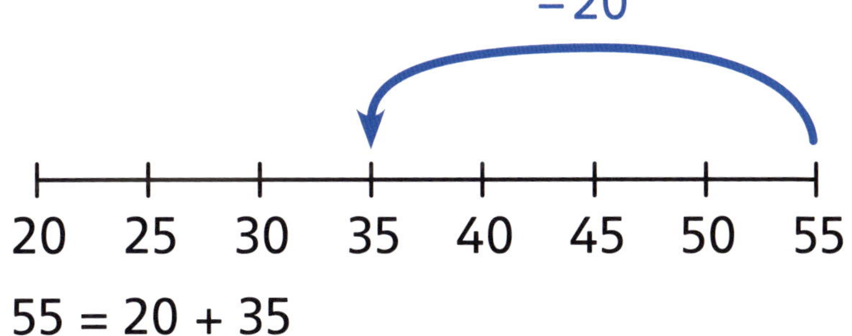

20   25   30   35   40   45   50   55

55 = 20 + 35

Marta had £35 before her father gave her £20.

b)

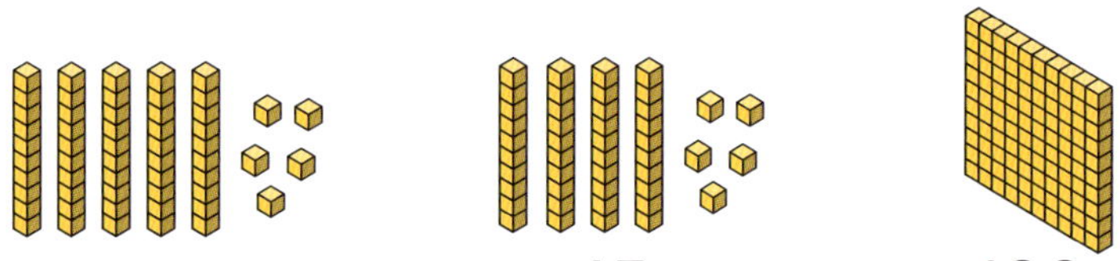

$$55 + 45 = 100$$

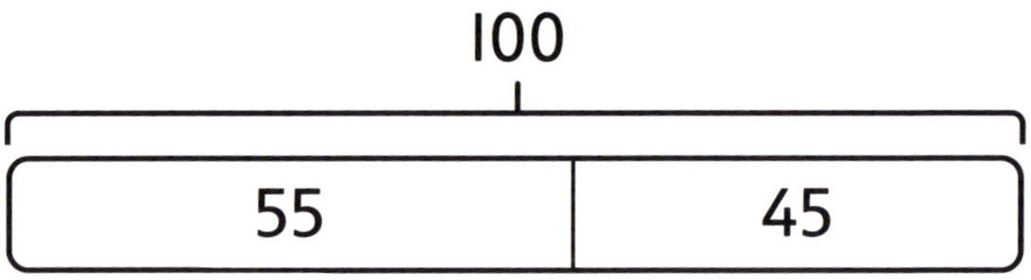

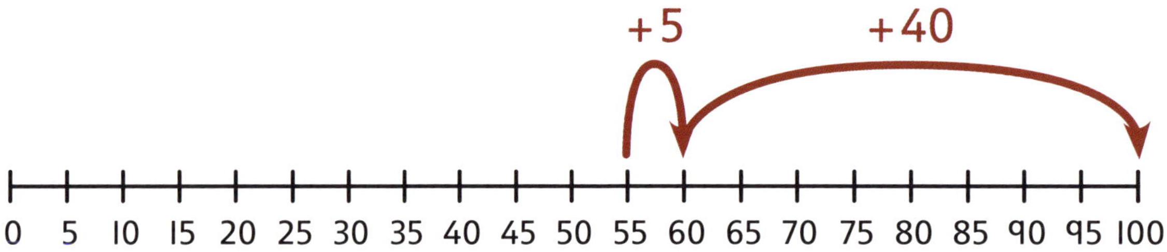

100

| 55 | 45 |

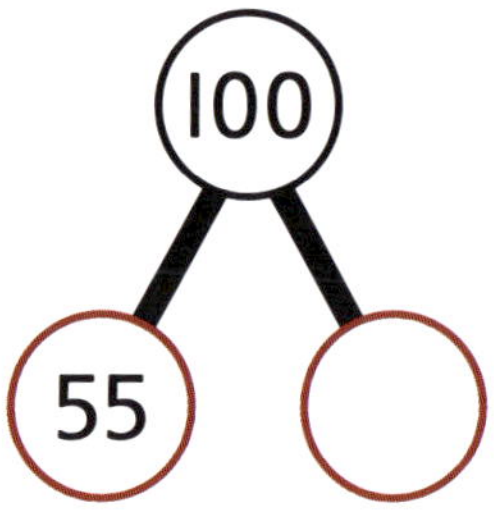

+5   +40

0 5 10 15 20 25 30 35 40 45 50 55 60 65 70 75 80 85 90 95 100

55 + 45 = 100
Marta needs to save another £45.

Think together

1 A box holds 40 cups. There are 18 cups on the table.
How many more cups are needed to fill the box?

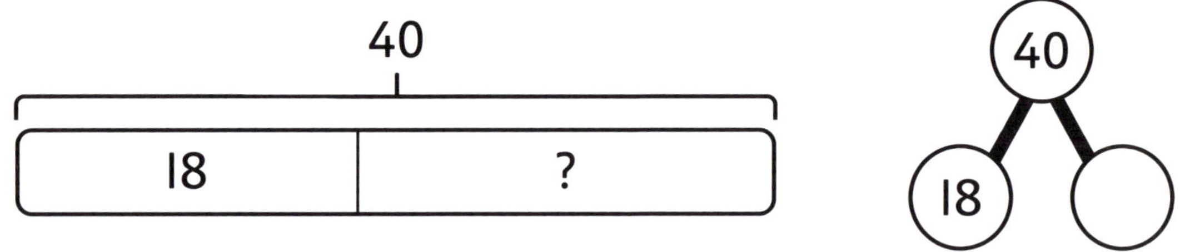

40

| 18 | ? |

2 A muffin costs 68p. Joe has 38p.

How much more does he need to buy a muffin?

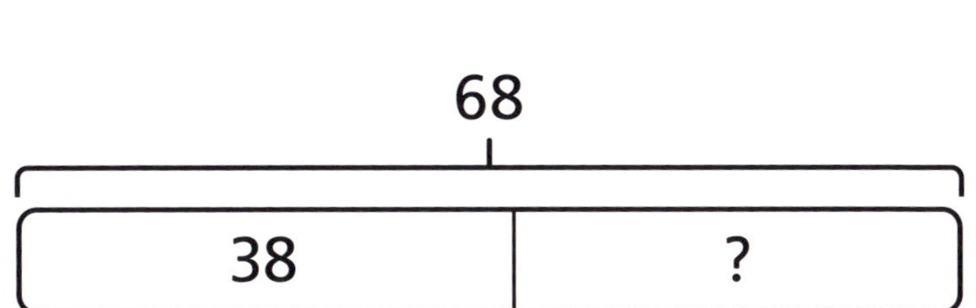

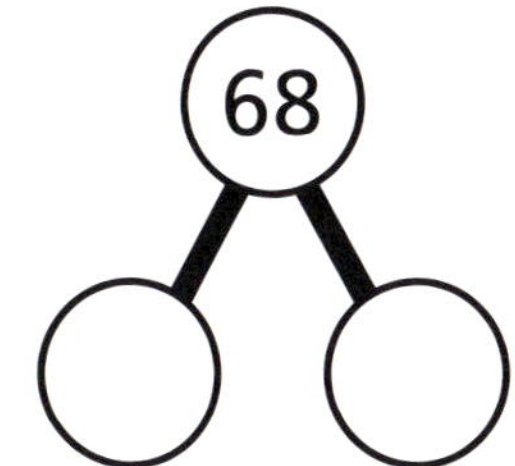

3 Find the value of ⭐ and complete the series of calculations.

$22 + ⭐ = 56$

$\square + ⭐ = 57$

$\square + ⭐ = 58$

$\square + ⭐ = 59$

$\square + ⭐ = 60$

103

Mental addition and subtraction ❶

Discover

❶ **a)** How old is Tim's brother?

b) How old is Tim's mum?

Share

a)

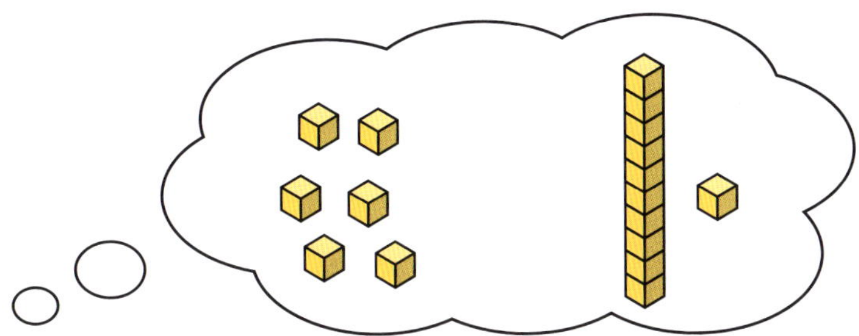

Add the 1s.

6 + 1 = 7 so

6 + 11 = 17

Tim's brother is 17 years old.

b) 6 + 31 = 37

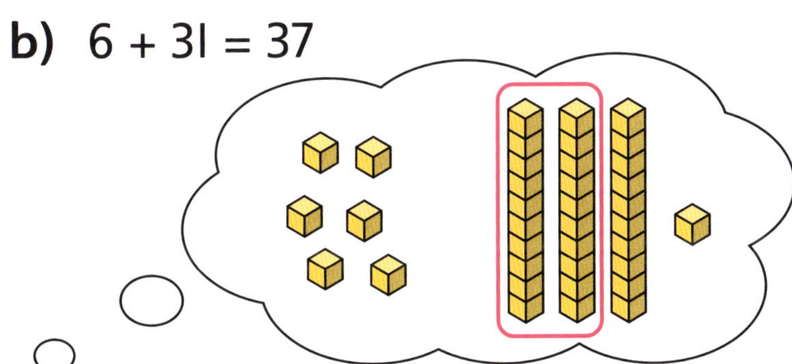

31 is 20 more than 11, so just add 20 to Tim's brother's age.

17 + 20 = 37

Tim's mum is 37 years old.

Think together

1 How old is Tim's grandma?

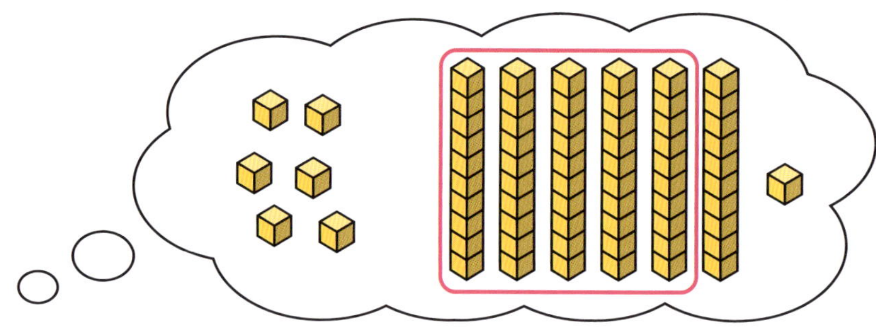

$6 + 61 = \boxed{}$

2 Tim's mum is 37 years old.

Tim's grandpa is 40 years older than Tim's mum.

How old is Tim's grandpa?

3

Look at these calculations.

Which ones can you do in your head?

25 + 4 = ☐   25 – 4 = ☐

42 + 30 = ☐   42 – 30 = ☐

36 + 7 = ☐   36 – 7 = ☐

28 + 12 = ☐   38 – 18 = ☐

Explain to a partner how you did them mentally.

107

Mental addition and subtraction ②

1 **a)** How much does a skateboard and a pair of knee-pads cost?

b) Ben buys a different skateboard and a helmet.

The total cost is £56.

How much does his skateboard cost?

Share

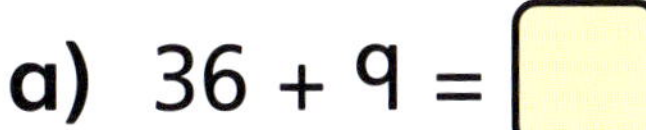

a) $36 + 9 = \boxed{}$

Count on in 1s: $36 + 9 = 45$

9 is one less than 10. Add 10 then subtract 1.

$36 + 9 = 36 + 10 - 1 = 45$

$£36 + £9 = £45$

A skateboard and a pair of knee-pads cost £45.

b) $56 - 19 = \boxed{}$

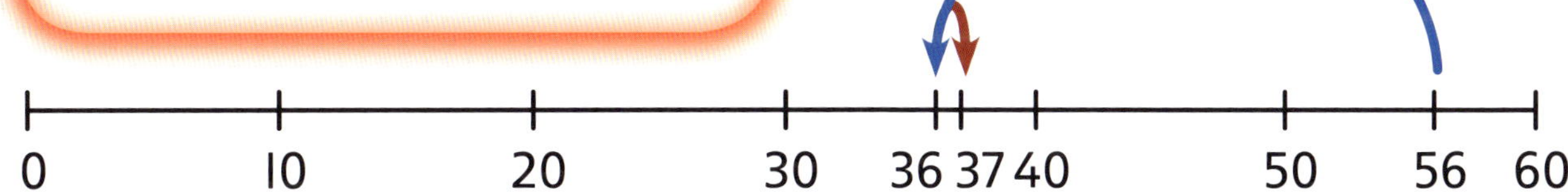

$56 - 19 = 56 - 20 + 1 = 37$

Ben's skateboard costs £37.

Think together

1 How much do a pair of roller blades at £54 and a helmet at £19 cost altogether?

1	2	3	4	5	6	7	8	9	10
11	12	13	14	15	16	17	18	19	20
21	22	23	24	25	26	27	28	29	30
31	32	33	34	35	36	37	38	39	40
41	42	43	44	45	46	47	48	49	50
51	52	53	54	55	56	57	58	59	60
61	62	63	64	65	66	67	68	69	70
71	72	73	74	75	76	77	78	79	80
81	82	83	84	85	86	87	88	89	90
91	92	93	94	95	96	97	98	99	100

$$54 + 19 = 54 + 20 - \boxed{} = \boxed{}$$

2 T-shirts are on sale. They cost £29 for two.

How much change will Lois get from £50?

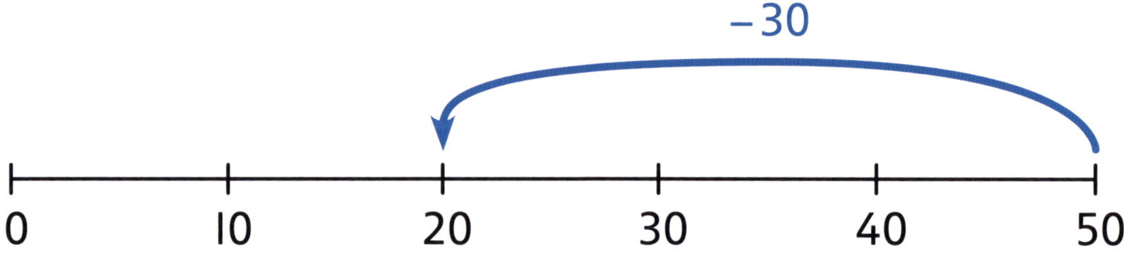

$$50 - 29 = 50 - \boxed{} + \boxed{} = \boxed{}$$

3 Kara and David are working out calculations in their heads.

What calculation are they each trying to work out?

$56 - \boxed{} = \boxed{}$

Kara

$37 + \boxed{} = \boxed{}$

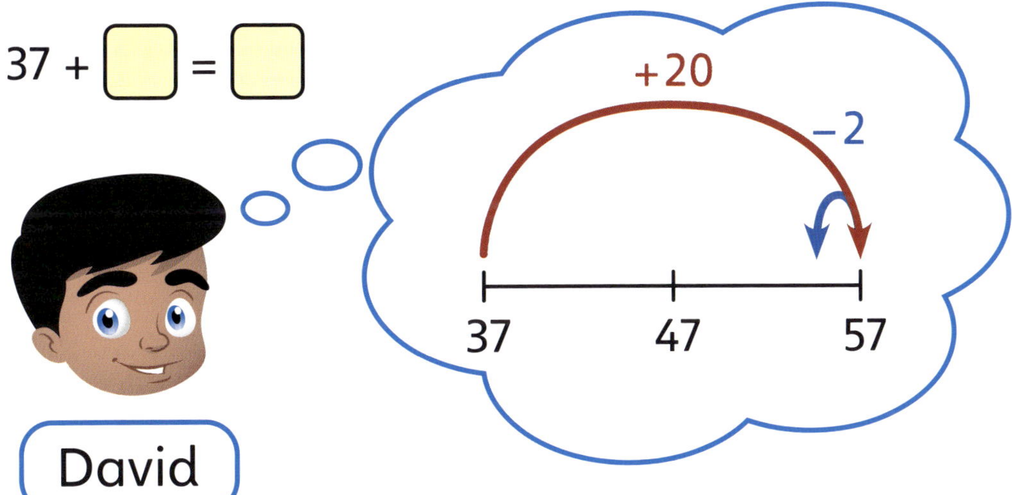

David

→ Practice book 2C p79

Efficient subtraction

Discover

1 **a)** What is the missing number?

△ – ◯ = ▢

b) What is the missing number?

△ – ■ = ▢

Share

a)

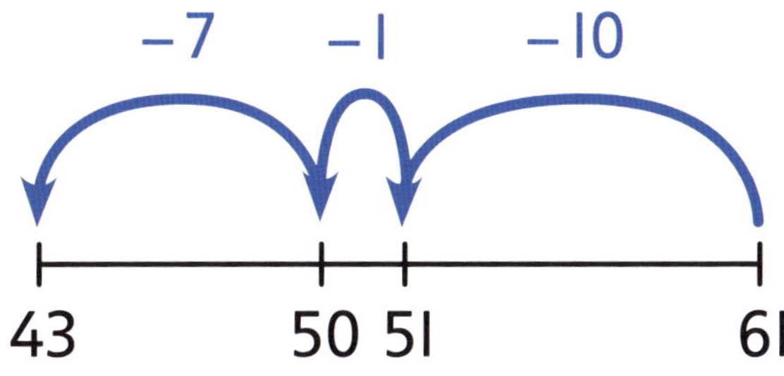

61 − 18 = 43

The missing number is 43.

b) Use a number line. First subtract 50 and then
subtract 6.

61 − 56 = 5

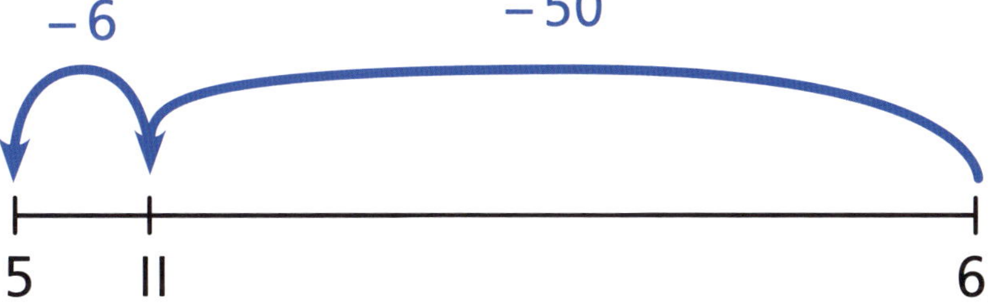

The missing number is 5.

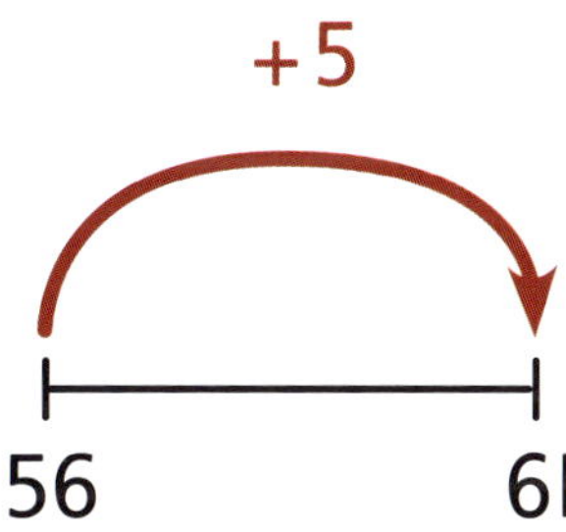

Think together

 **1**

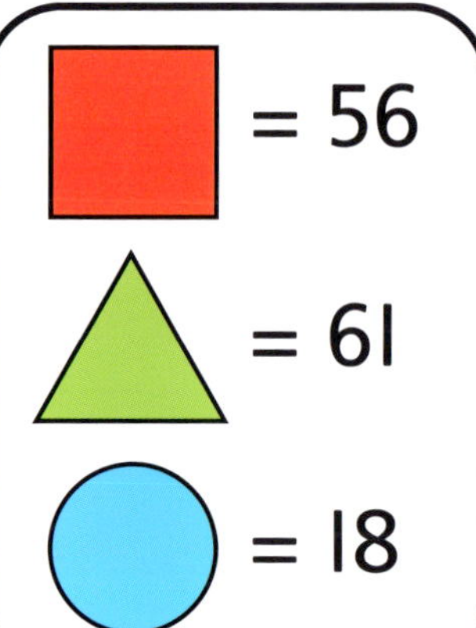

Choose your own method to solve this.

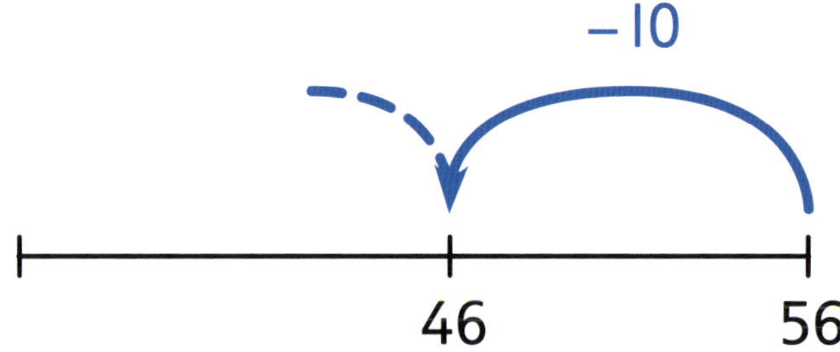

2 Work out:

$56 - 49 = \boxed{}$ $56 - 47 = \boxed{}$

$56 - 48 = \boxed{}$ $56 - 46 = \boxed{}$

What do you notice about the answers?

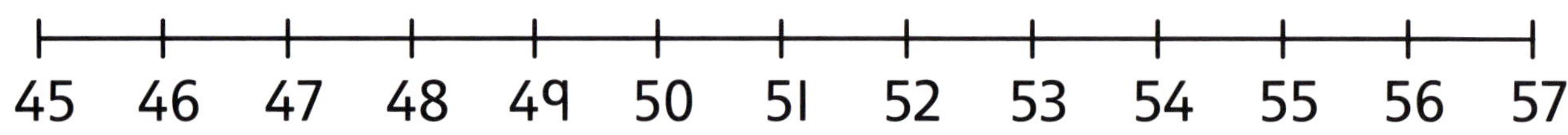

3

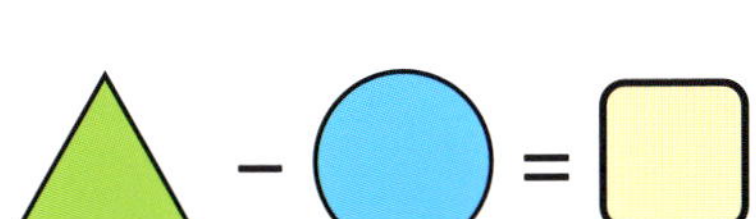

$\triangle = 81$ $\bigcirc = 72$

$\blacksquare = 8$ $\bigstar = 48$

$\triangle - \bigcirc = \square$

$\bigstar - \blacksquare = \square$

$\triangle - \blacksquare = \square$

$\bigcirc - \square = \bigstar$

What different methods would you use to solve these?

Discuss with a partner which methods you think suit the problems best.

Do you agree?

115

→ **Practice book 2C p82**

Solve problems – addition and subtraction

Discover

1 **a)** How much does a cup of tea and a teacake cost altogether?

b) 1 egg + 1 piece of toast = 74p

2 eggs + 1 piece of toast = £1

How much does one piece of toast cost?

Share

a) A cup of tea costs 40p.

A teacake costs 58p.

40p + 58p = 98p

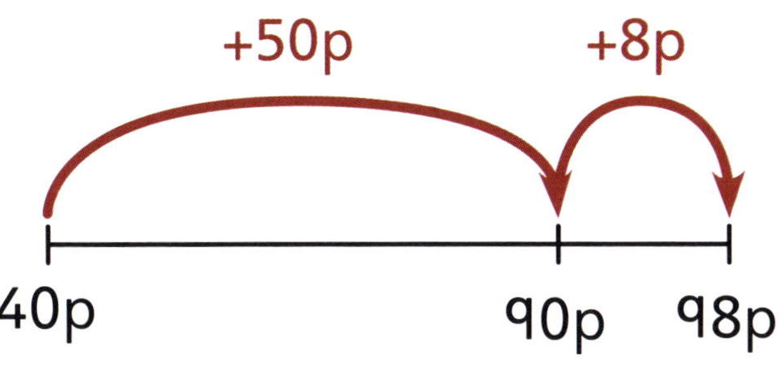

A cup of tea and a teacake cost 98p altogether.

b) There is one more egg on one plate.

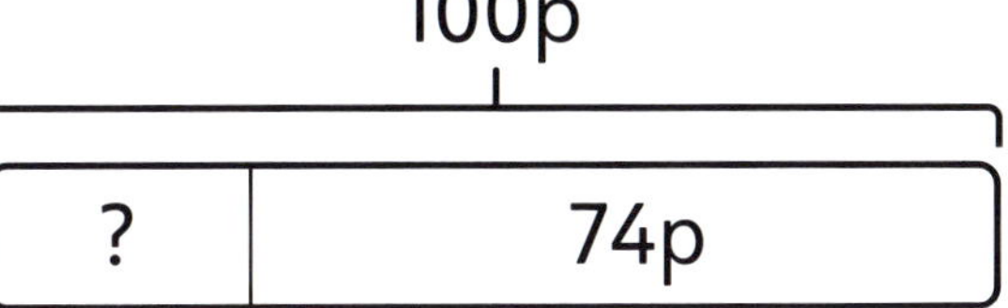

100p − 74p = 26p

So one egg costs 26p.

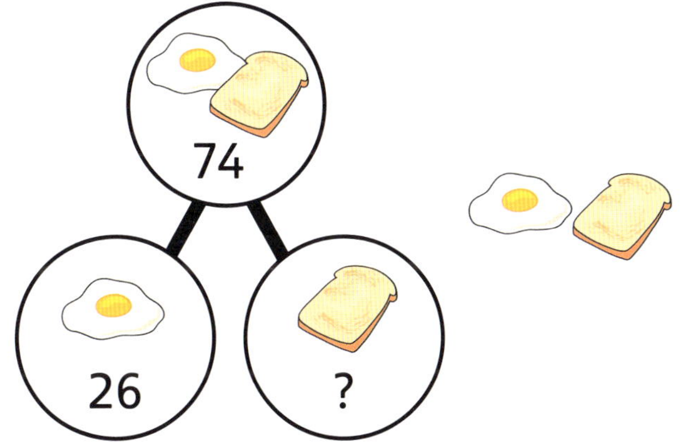

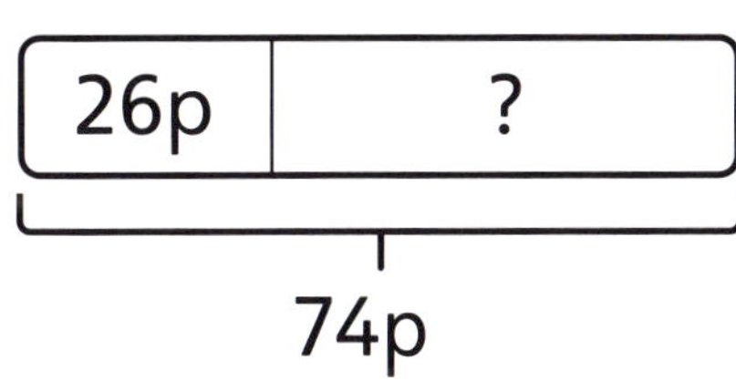

74p − 26p = 48p

One piece of toast costs 48p.

Think together

1 How much more does a teacake cost than an egg?

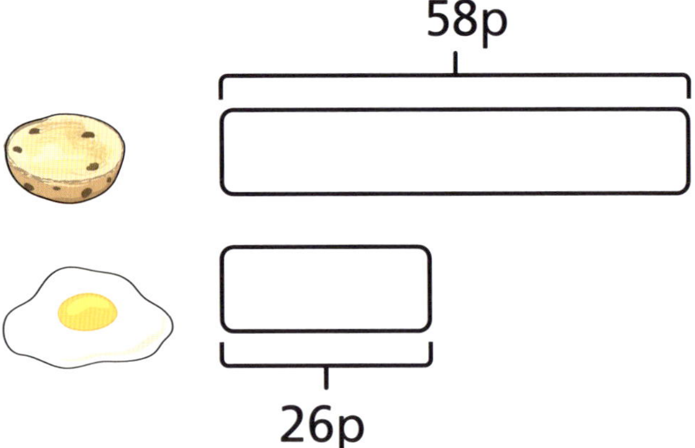

58p

26p

Cup of tea: 40p

Teacake: 58p

Egg: 26p

Toast: 48p

2 Filip buys a cup of tea and an egg.

Filip pays with   .

How much change does he get?

70p		
40p	26p	?

3 Josh has some blocks.

He uses them to make these.

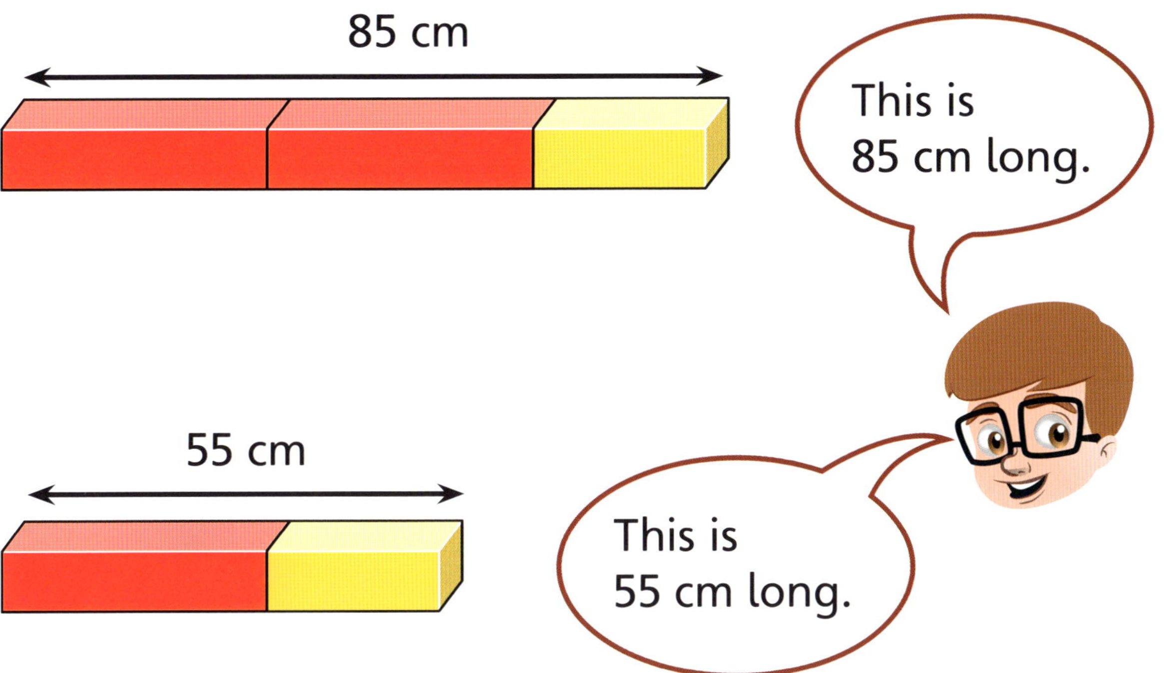

How long is each block?

119

Solve problems – multiplication and division

Discover

1 a) Erik buys four snorkel and mask sets.
What is the total cost?

b) Six beach balls cost £12.
How much do three beach balls cost?

Share

a)

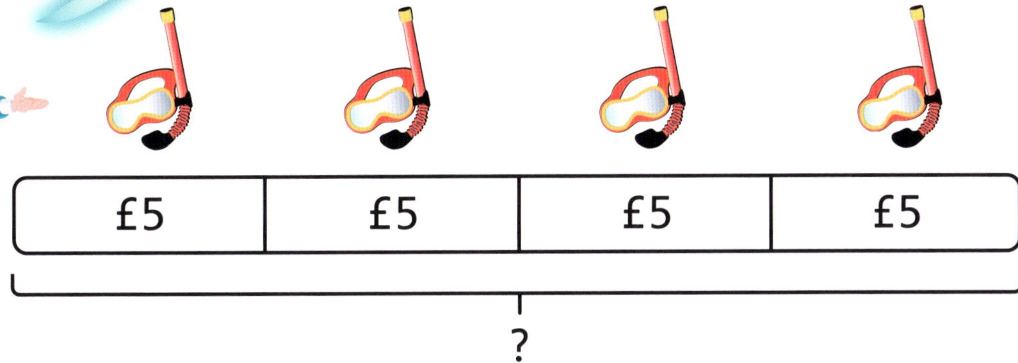

£5 × 4 = £20

The total cost is £20.

b) Work out the cost of one beach ball.

£12 ÷ 6 = £2

Each beach ball costs £2.

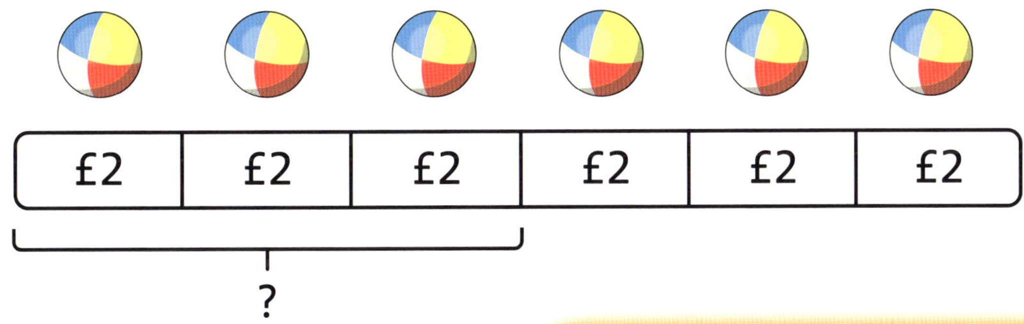

£2 × 3 = £6

Three beach balls cost £6.

I knew that the cost of three beach balls is half of the cost of six beach balls, so I halved £12.

Think together

1 Eric buys 10 pairs of flippers.

How many flippers are there altogether?

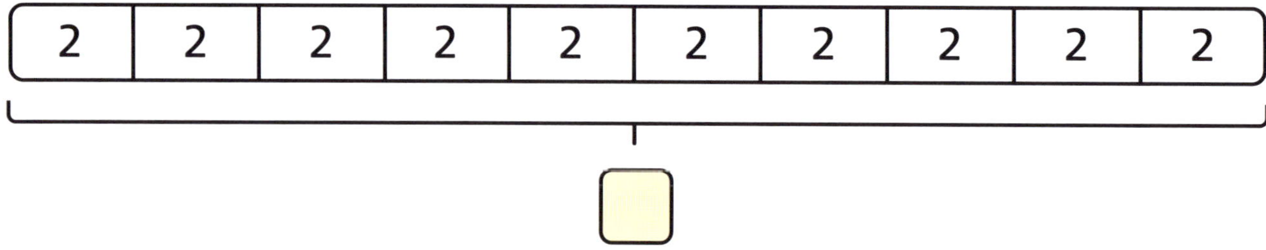

2 5 pairs of sunglasses cost £30.

How much does one pair of sunglasses cost?

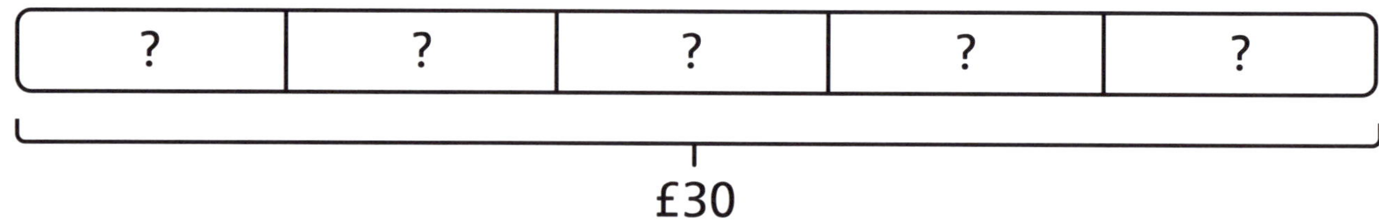

3 Shay and Amy buy these ice lollies.

They share them equally.

How many do they each get?

I will draw them and share them out one by one.

I don't think you need to share them one by one. I think there is a quicker way.

123

→ **Practice book 2C p88**

Solve problems – using the four operations

Discover

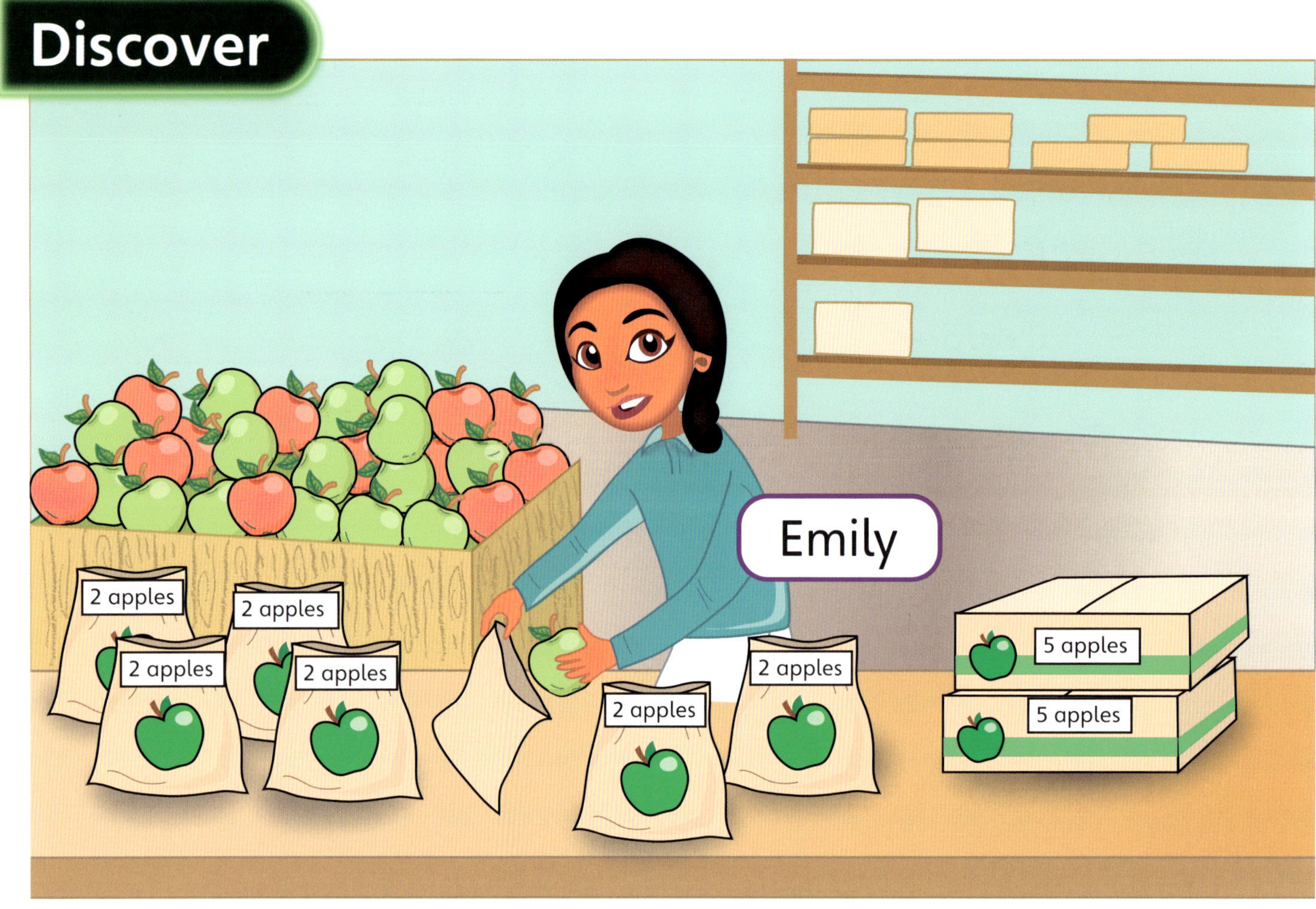

1 **a)** How many apples are there altogether in the full bags and boxes?

b) Emily has 25 more apples to put into boxes.

Each box can hold five apples. She fills three boxes.

How many apples are left?

Share

a) There are six bags of two apples.

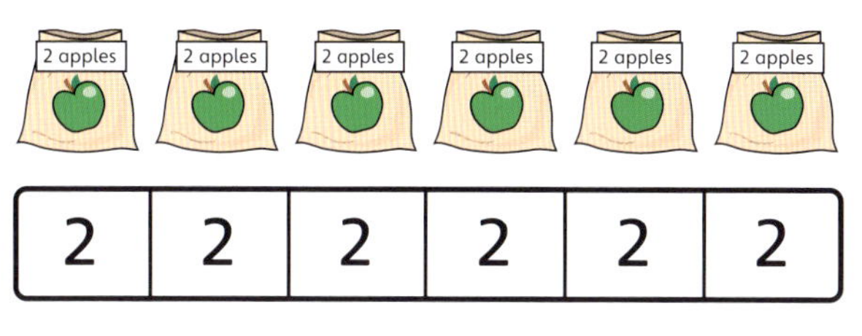

$6 \times 2 = 12$ apples

There are two boxes of five apples.

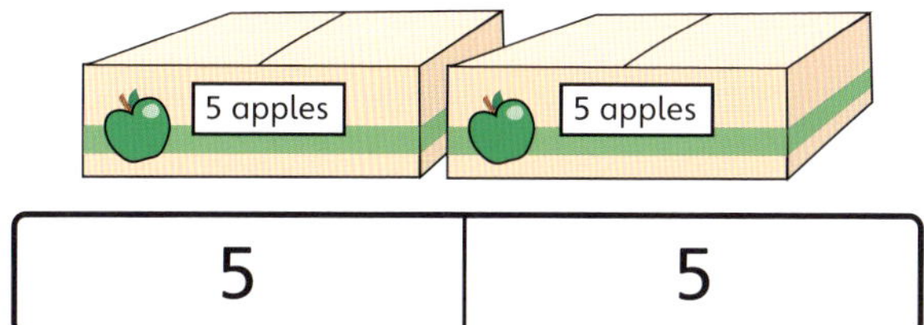

$2 \times 5 = 10$ apples

$12 + 10 = 22$ apples

There are 22 apples altogether.

b) Work out how many apples Emily has packed and then subtract this from the total number of apples to find the difference.

$3 \times 5 = 15$ apples

$25 - 15 = 10$

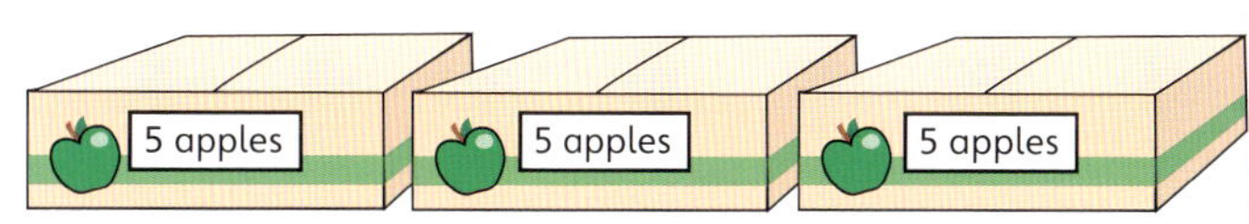

25			
5	5	5	

$25 - 5 - 5 - 5 = 10$

There are 10 apples left.

Think together

1

How much does the rice cost in total?

| 10 | 10 | 10 | 2 | 2 | 2 | 2 |

2 Mantas has £20.

How much money does he have left after buying two small bags of rice?

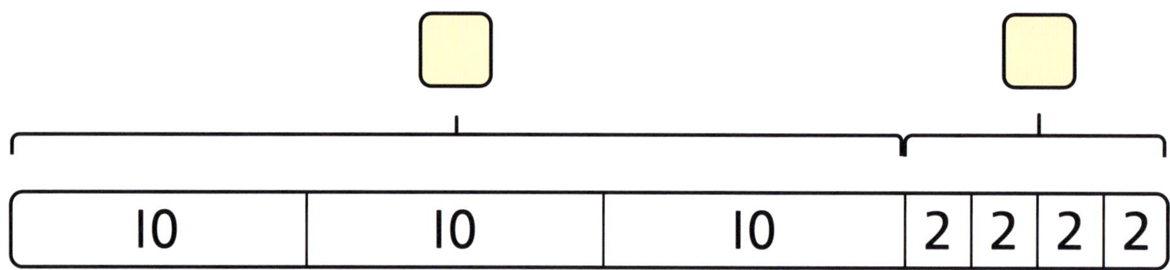

20		
2	2	?

3 Liam has £30.

He buys these bags of rice.

How many small bags of rice can he buy with the change?

→ Practice book 2C p91

End of unit check

1 Adam is saving for a new game.

Adam saved £40 in January.

He saved £30 in February.

How much more money does he need to save?

A £70 **B** £10 **C** £30 **D** £60

2 Which pair of numbers **cannot** go in the boxes to make the calculation correct.

1☐ + ☐ = 23

A 10 and 13 **B** 5 and 8 **C** 8 and 5 **D** 3 and 10

3 Paul has a rope that is 50 m long.

He cuts it into two equal parts.

Which calculation shows the length of each piece?

A 50 + 2 **B** 50 − 2 **C** 50 × 2 **D** 50 ÷ 2

 **4** Hanna has 60 grapes.

She gives 32 to Scott. She gives 15 to Amir.

How many grapes does Hanna have left?

A 13　　　　　**B** 47　　　　　**C** 28　　　　　**D** 17

Think!

Explain the steps you need to solve this question.

Oranges are packed into boxes of 4.

I have 10 boxes of oranges.

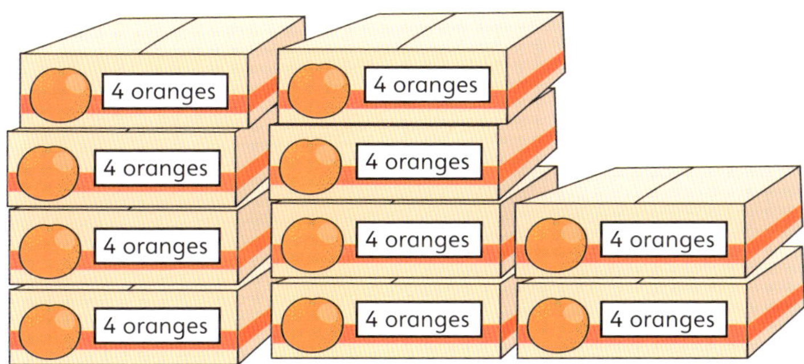

The oranges are then put into bags of 5.

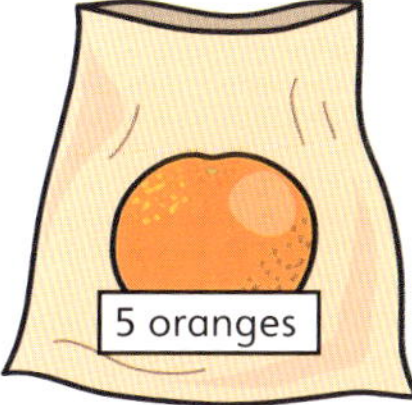

How many bags of 5 oranges will I have?

→ **Practice book 2C p94**

Unit 13
Position and direction

In this unit we will …
- ⚡ Describe movement
- ⚡ Describe turns
- ⚡ Make patterns by turning shapes

We will use shapes to make patterns. Can you say which shape has made a half turn?

clockwise

anticlockwise

forwards

backwards

left

right

middle

turn

half turn

quarter turn

three-quarter turn

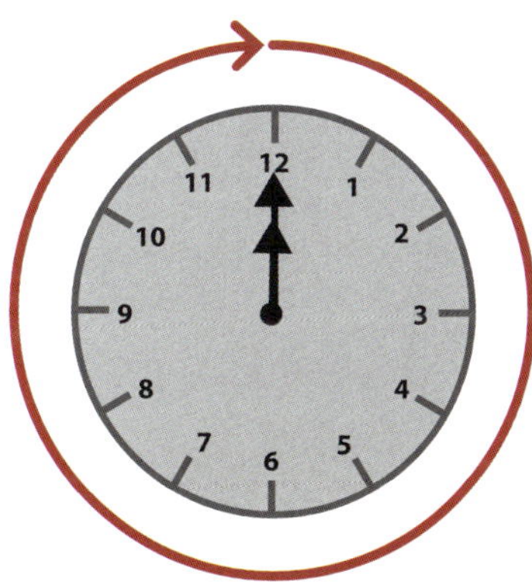

Language of position

Discover

1 a) Describe the scene using some of these words: above, next to, over, under.

b) Describe the scene using some of these words: below, between, beneath, behind.

Share

a)

The lorry is above the boat.

The duck is next to a sheep.

The birds are over the tree.

The boat is under the bridge.

b)

The sun is behind a cloud.

The duck is between the two sheep.

The tree is below the birds.

The boat is beneath the bridge.

I can see that under, below and beneath all mean the same thing.

Think together

1 Use the words **left**, **middle** and **right** to describe the view.

2 Choose an item.

Describe its position using words from the word list.

top

middle

bottom

between

beside

left

right

3 Play a game with a partner.

You need some toys or shapes.

Arrange them in positions, to make a scene, but keep them hidden from your partner.

Describe the positions to your partner.

Can they make the same scene?

→ **Practice book 2C p96**

Describe movement

Discover

1 a) Follow the instructions on the screen to complete the dance.

b) Describe the movements in the dance.

Share

a) and **b)** These are the movements in the dance.

Step 1: forwards

Step 4: forwards

Step 2: backwards

Step 5: right

Step 3: left

Step 6: forwards

Think together

1 Here are three sandcastles.

Complete the sentences.

The ______________ flag is in the middle.

The green triangle flag is to the right of the ______________ flag.

The ______________ flag is to the right of the green triangle flag.

2 Complete the sentences.

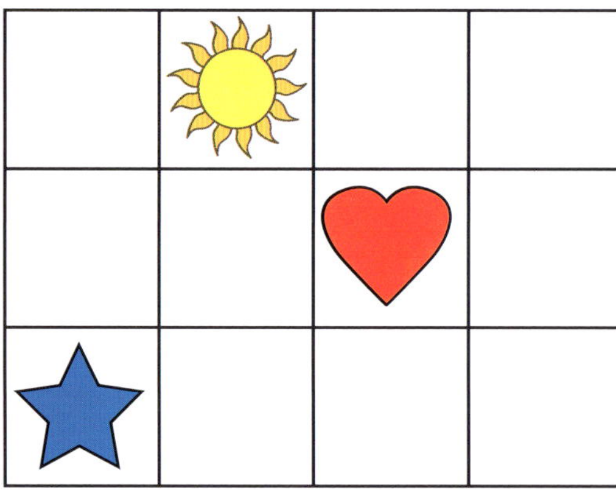

a) To move from the heart to the sun, move ☐ square up and ☐ square left.

b) Describe how to move from the star to the sun.

Can you do this in more than one way?

3 Jake the mouse is in one of the squares in the field.

Jake moves away from the entrance:

I square forwards

I square left

I square backwards

I square right.

Where does Jake finish?

→ **Practice book 2C p99**

Describe turns

Discover

1 **a)** Sam is facing the goat.

She makes a half turn.

What is Sam facing now?

b) Sam faces the cow.

She makes a quarter turn left.

What is she facing now?

Share

a)

Sam is facing the cow now.

b)

Sam is facing the horse now.

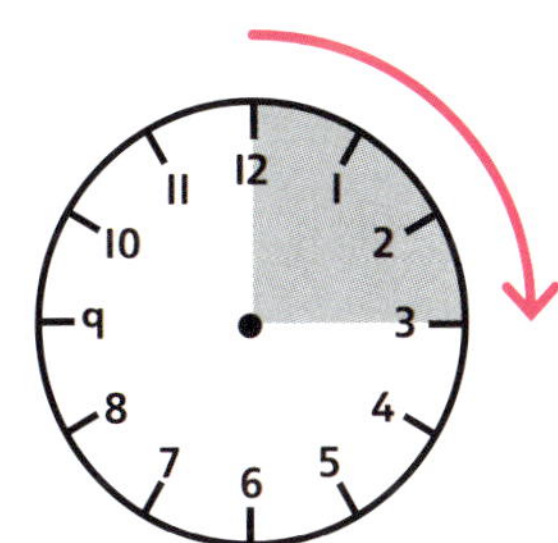

Think together

1 Choose clockwise or anticlockwise to describe how Sam turns.

a) Goat to hen is a quarter turn

____________ .

b) Horse to cow is a **three-quarter**

turn ____________ .

c) Hen to hen is a whole turn

____________ .

2 Match each picture to the correct description.

Three-quarter turn clockwise

Quarter turn clockwise

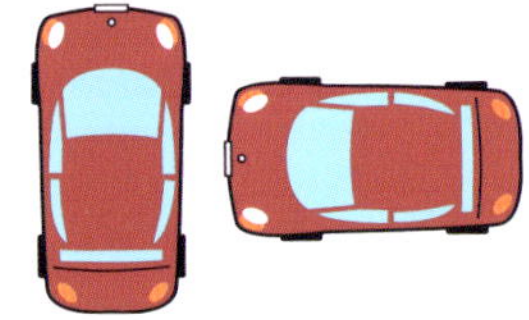

Half turn anticlockwise

3

Harry   **Amelia**   **Dai**

Who is correct? Explain why.

143

→ Practice book 2C p102

Describe movement and turns

Discover

1 **a)** Help the pirate reach the treasure safely.

Write instructions to get him to the treasure.

b) From the treasure, the pirate moves forwards 1, makes a quarter turn anticlockwise, then moves forwards 2.

Where is he now?

Share

To get the treasure, the pirate needs to move:

a)

forwards 2   quarter turn clockwise   forwards 1

b)

forwards 1   quarter turn anticlockwise   forwards 2

Think together

1 Put the sentences in the correct order to show how the pirate can get to the treasure chest. Use 1st, 2nd, 3rd.

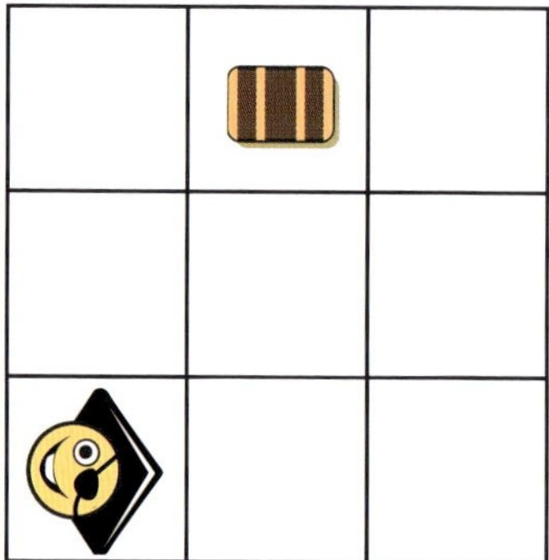

Go forwards 2 spaces.

Make a quarter turn anticlockwise.

Go forwards 1 space.

2 Complete the sentences to describe how the pirate can get to the treasure chest.

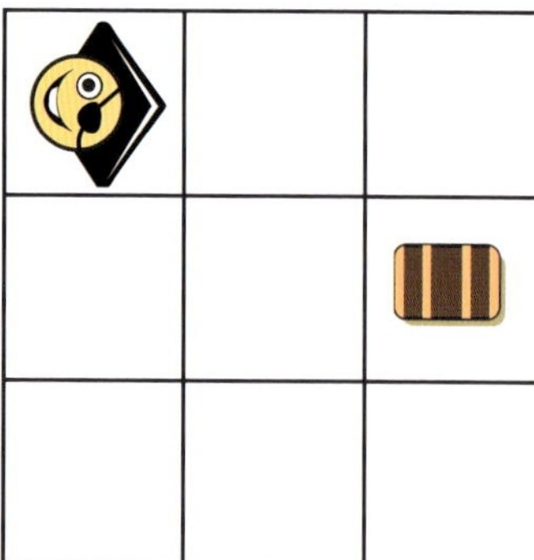

Go _____________ ⬜ spaces.

Make a _____________ turn _____________ .

Go _____________ ⬜ space.

3

If the pirate follows the instructions, where will he be?

I step forwards

Quarter turn anticlockwise

2 steps forwards

Three-quarter turn anticlockwise

I step forwards

Can you make up
your own story to get
to a different place?

147

→ Practice book 2C p105

Make patterns by turning shapes

Discover

1 **a)** What will the next two shapes in the pattern be?

b) What is the same about the shapes in the pattern?

What is different?

Share

a) The next two shapes will be

b) All the shapes are triangles.

They all have three sides.

They are all the same size and colour.

The triangles are in a different position. They have made a half turn after each shape in the pattern.

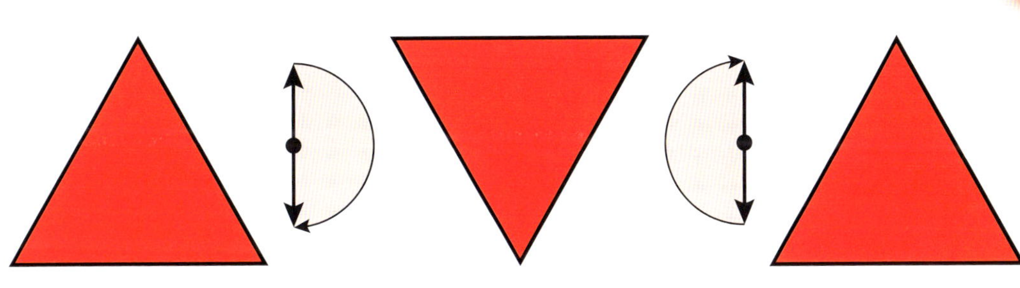

Think together

1 a) Point to the shape that comes next in the pattern.

b) Describe the turn it makes.

2 What is the missing shape?

3 What will the next three shapes in the pattern be?

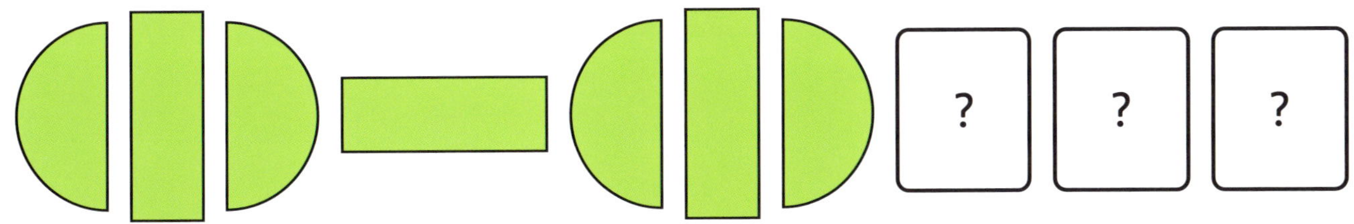

→ **Practice book 2C p108**

End of unit check

1 Which sentence **does not** describe the turn?

   A Quarter turn clockwise

   B Three-quarter turn anticlockwise

   C Quarter turn anticlockwise

   D Quarter turn right

2 Which instructions will get the man to the boat?

   A Forwards 3, quarter turn anticlockwise, forwards 1

   B Forwards 3, quarter turn clockwise, forwards 1

   C Forwards 3, quarter turn left, forwards 1

   D Quarter turn right, forwards 1, quarter turn left, forwards 2

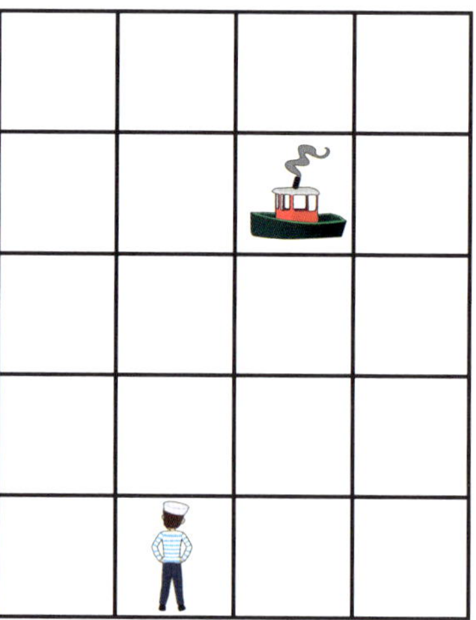

3 Describe how the heart shape turns to make the pattern.

 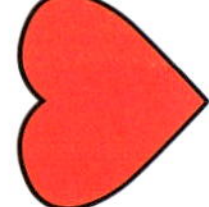  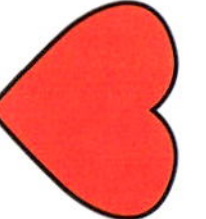  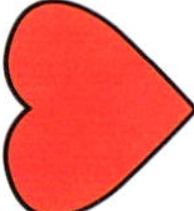  

   A Half turn

   C Whole turn

   B Quarter turn anticlockwise

   D Quarter turn clockwise

4 Which image completes the pattern?

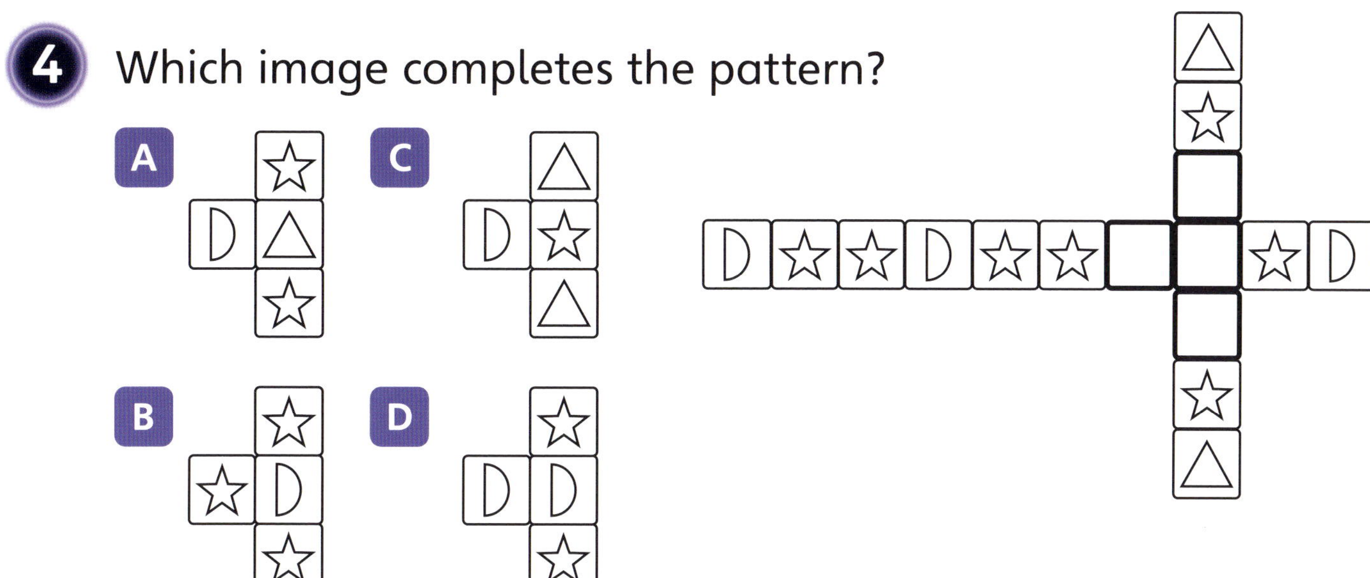

Think!

Ask a partner to choose an item.

Write some questions you could ask to work out which item they have chosen.

For example: Is it on the top row?

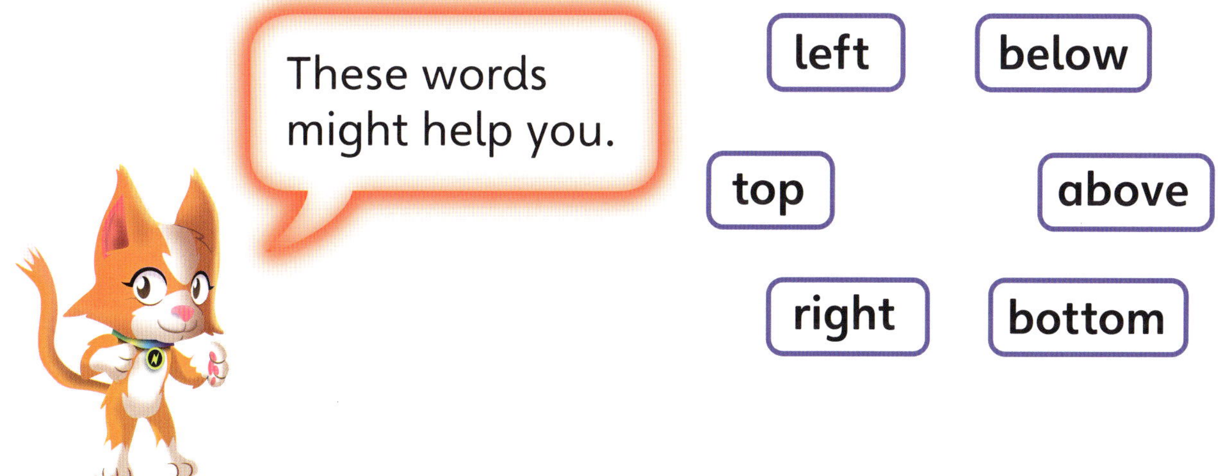

left   below

top   above

right   bottom

→ Practice book 2C p111

Unit 14
Statistics

tally chart   pictogram
key   table   block diagram

Name	Number
Tariq	🍎🍎🍎🍎🍎🍎🍎🍎🍎🍎
Amy	🍎🍎🍎🍎🍎🍎🍎

Make tally charts

Discover

1 **a)** Tariq and Amy are playing a game.

How many games did each child win?

b) Who won overall? Tariq or Amy? How do you know?

Share

a) Count Tariq's tally marks.

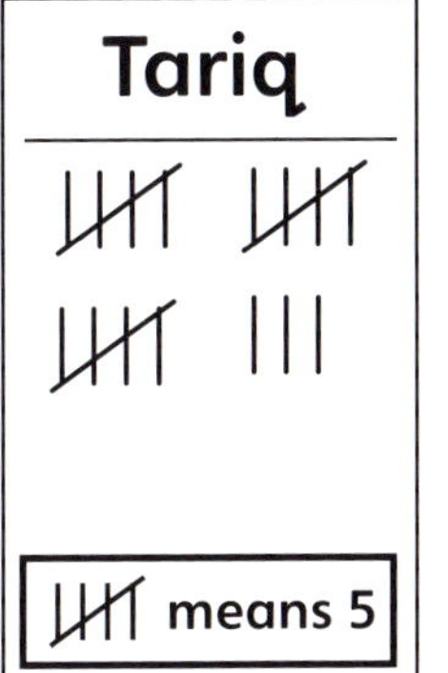

Tariq won 18 games.

Count Amy's tally marks.

Amy won 24 games.

b)

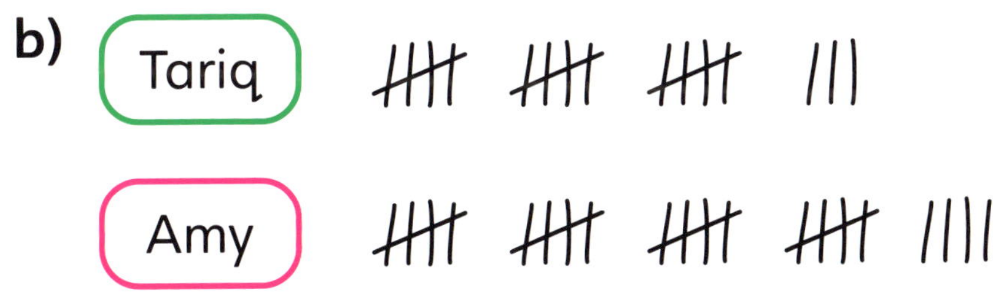

Amy won overall. 24 is greater than 18.

Think together

1 These choices have been tallied in a **tally chart**.

Write the tally number for each choice.

Choice	Tally	Number
✊	|||| |||| |||	
✋	|||| |||| ||||	
✌	|||| |||| ||	

2 Here are some red buttons, yellow cubes and blue counters.

a) Create a tally chart to show how many of each colour.

b) Which item is there the greatest number of?

c) Which item is there the least number of?

3 Max counts the number of counters, pencils and rulers on his desk.

The tally chart shows how many of each he has.

Object	Tally
⬤ (red counter)	ⅢⅢ ⅢⅢ ‖
▬▬▬▶ (pencil)	ⅢⅢ ‖
ruler	‖‖‖

Gather objects from the classroom to match this tally chart.

159

Tables

Discover

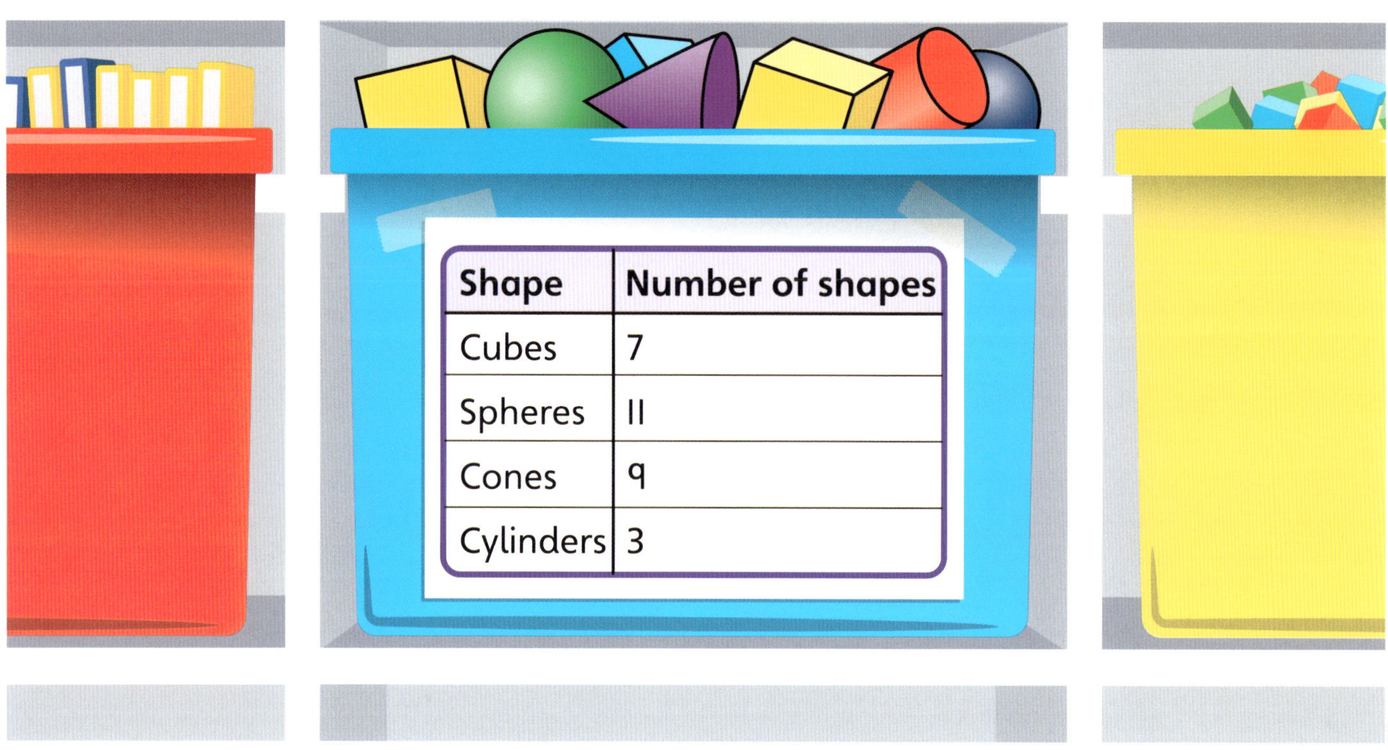

1 **a)** How many cones are in the box?

b) The teacher puts 5 more cubes into the box.

How many cubes are in the box now?

Share

a)

Shape	Number of shapes
Cubes	7
Spheres	11
Cones	9
Cylinders	3

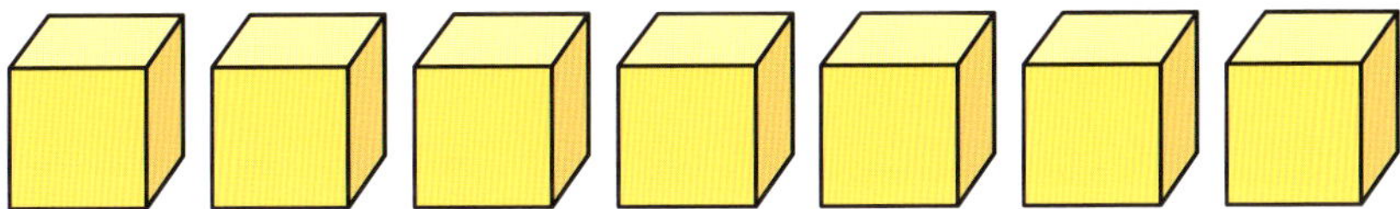

There are 9 cones in the box.

b) There are 7 cubes in the box already.

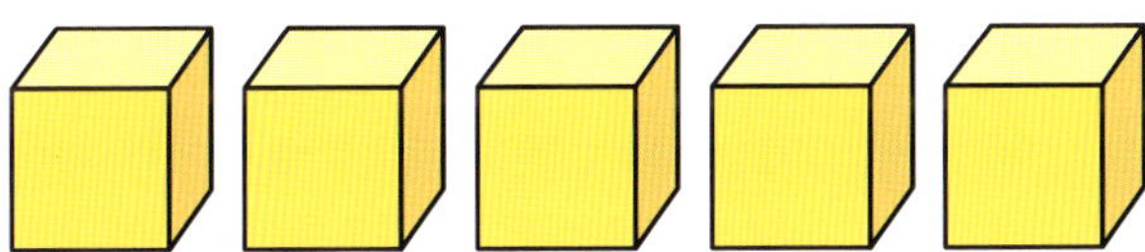

5 more are added to the box.

$7 + 5 = 12$

There are 12 cubes in the box now.

Think together

1   Here is a box of sports equipment.

Name	Number
Footballs	6
Bats	10
Cones	6
Ropes	5

How many of each item are in the box?

2   Here is another box of toys.

Name	Number
Cars	5
Teddies	7
Planes	3

How many toys are in the box in total?

3 Harry has 10 letter tiles.

The table shows how many of each letter he has.

Letter	Number
A	2
D	1
E	3
R	1
T	2
S	1

a) How many As and Es does he have in total?

b) Which letter does he have most of?

c) Which letters does he only have one of?

d) Make a word with some of Harry's letters.

163

Block diagrams

Discover

I **a)** Who has the most points?

How do you know?

b) Which children have the same number of points?

How do you know?

Share

a) Count each score in 1s.

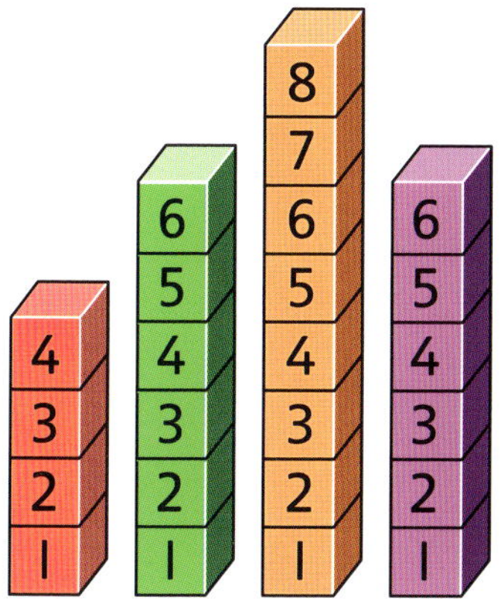

Izzy	4
Joe	6
Jack	8
Kara	6

Use the scale on the side and compare the height of the towers.

This is called a **block diagram**.

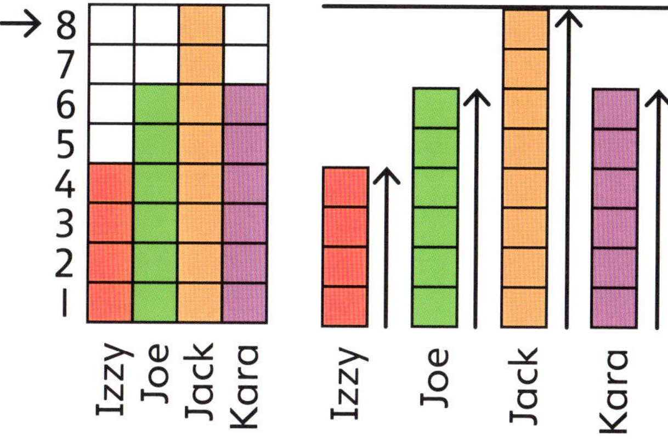

Jack has the most points as he has the highest tower.

b) Use the scale on the side to see which scores are the same.

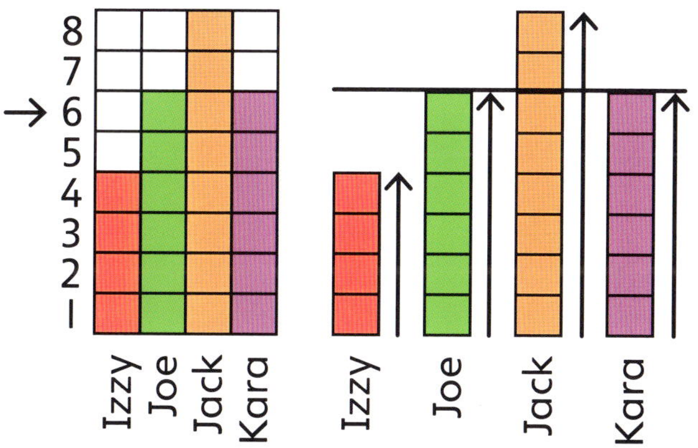

Joe and Kara have the same number of points.

Think together

1 The children in Class 2 are put into teams for a quiz.

Here are the results.

a) Which team scored the most points?

How do you know?

b) Which team scored the fewest points?

How do you know?

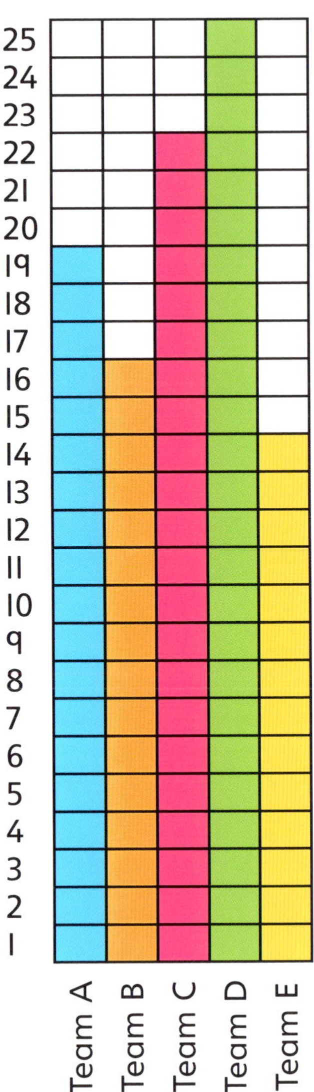

2 Use cubes to make a block diagram of these sports day team results.

3 Three children are discussing favourite animals.

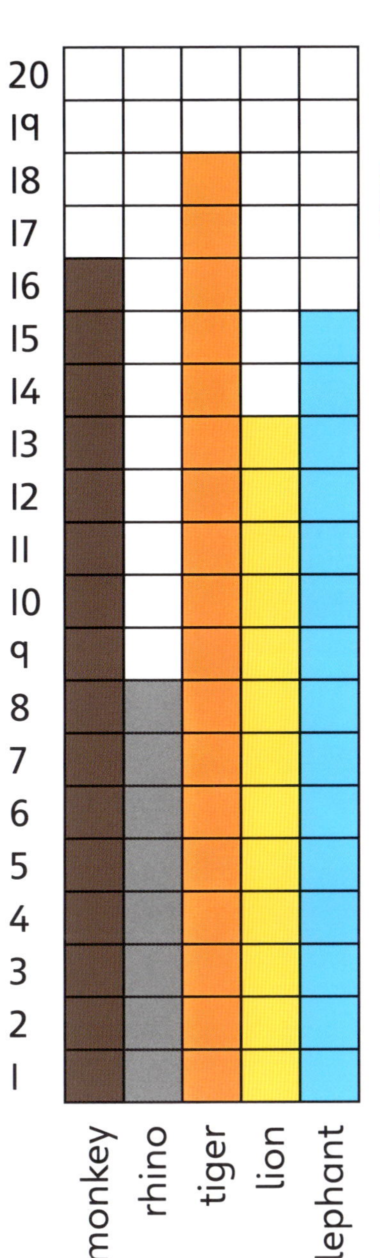

a) Are all the children correct?

b) Create your own fact for this block diagram.

→ **Practice book 2C p119**

Draw pictograms (1 to 1)

Discover

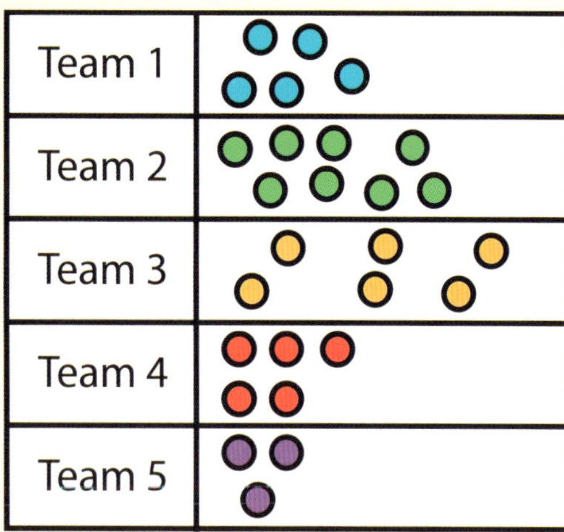

1   a) Line up the points for each team in the table.

    b) Which team got the most points?

        How many points did they get?

Share

a)

Team 1	● ● ● ● ●
Team 2	● ● ● ● ● ● ● ●
Team 3	● ● ● ● ● ●
Team 4	● ● ● ● ●
Team 5	● ● ●

Each ◯ represents 1 team point.

b) Team 2 has the most points.
It has 8 points.

Think together

1 20 children are asked how they travel to school.

Here are the results.

How child travels to school	Number of children
walk	9
car	3
bike	6
other	2

Complete the pictogram for this data.

walk	☺ ☺ ☺ ☺ ☺ ☺ ☺ ☺ ☺
car	
bike	
other	

Each ☺ represents 1 child.

2   Arun has drawn a pictogram to show how many animals he has.

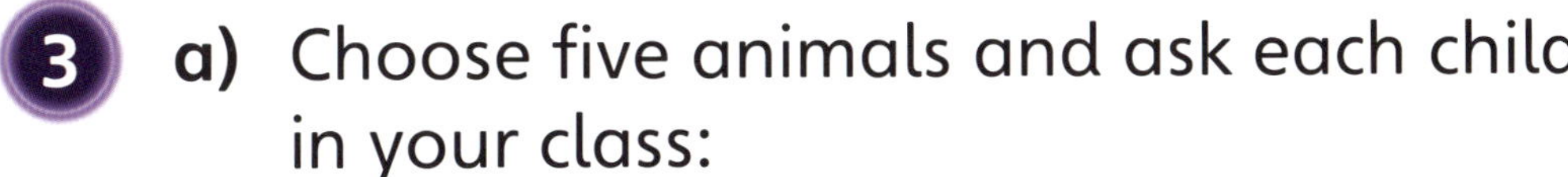

Animal	
cat	
dog	
fish	

What is wrong with Arun's pictogram?

3   **a)**   Choose five animals and ask each child in your class:

Which is your favourite animal?

b)   Collect your results in a tally chart.

c)   Draw a pictogram for your tally chart.

171

Interpret pictograms (I to I)

Discover

crab 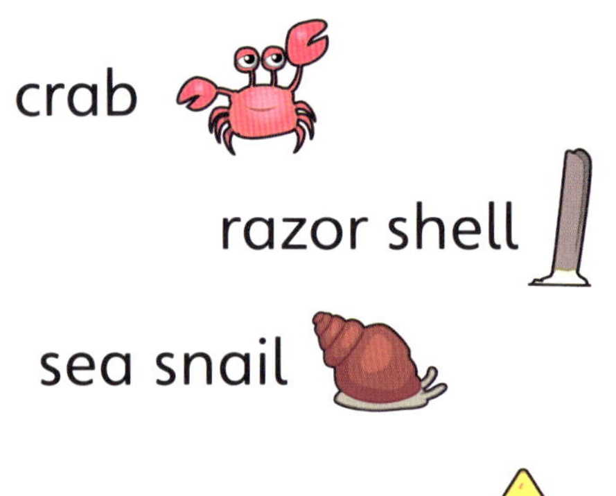

razor shell

sea snail

starfish

shrimp 

Creature	Number of creatures
	●●●●
	●●●●●●●●
	●●●●●●
	●●
	●●●●●●●●●●

Each ● represents I creature.

I **a)** Some children make a pictogram to show how many creatures they have found.

The labels are missing from the pictogram.

Work out where each label should go.

b) Which creature did the children find most of?

Share

a) First count how many of each creature there are.

Creature	Number of creatures
crab	4
sea snail	8
shrimp	6
razor shell	2
starfish	10

Then complete the pictogram.

Creature	Number of creatures
crab	●●●●
sea snail	●●●●●●●●
shrimp	●●●●●●
razor shell	●●
starfish	●●●●●●●●●●

Each ● represents 1 creature.

b) There were 10 starfish.

The children found most starfish.

Think together

1 This pictogram shows the number of hours of sunshine on three different days.

Day	Hours of sunshine
Monday	☀ ☀ ☀ ☀
Tuesday	☀ ☀ ☀ ☀ ☀ ☀ ☀
Wednesday	☀

Each ☀ represents 1 hour.

a) Which day had the most sunshine?

b) Which day has the least sunshine?

c) How many hours of sunshine were there on Tuesday?

d) How many more hours of sunshine were there on Monday than Wednesday?

2 Write down 3 things you know from this pictogram.

Each ☺ represents 1 child.

Team	Number in team
boys	☺ ☺ ☺ ☺ ☺ ☺
girls	☺ ☺ ☺ ☺ ☺

3 This pictogram shows the number of monster stickers that four children have.

Child	Number of stickers
Tom	(7 monster stickers)
Sam	(5 monster stickers)
Kim	(3 monster stickers)
Mo	(5 monster stickers)

Which two children have the same number of stickers?

Which child has the fewest stickers?

Use the pictogram to make up your own question for a partner.

→ **Practice book 2C p125**

Draw pictograms (1 to 2, 5 or 10)

Discover

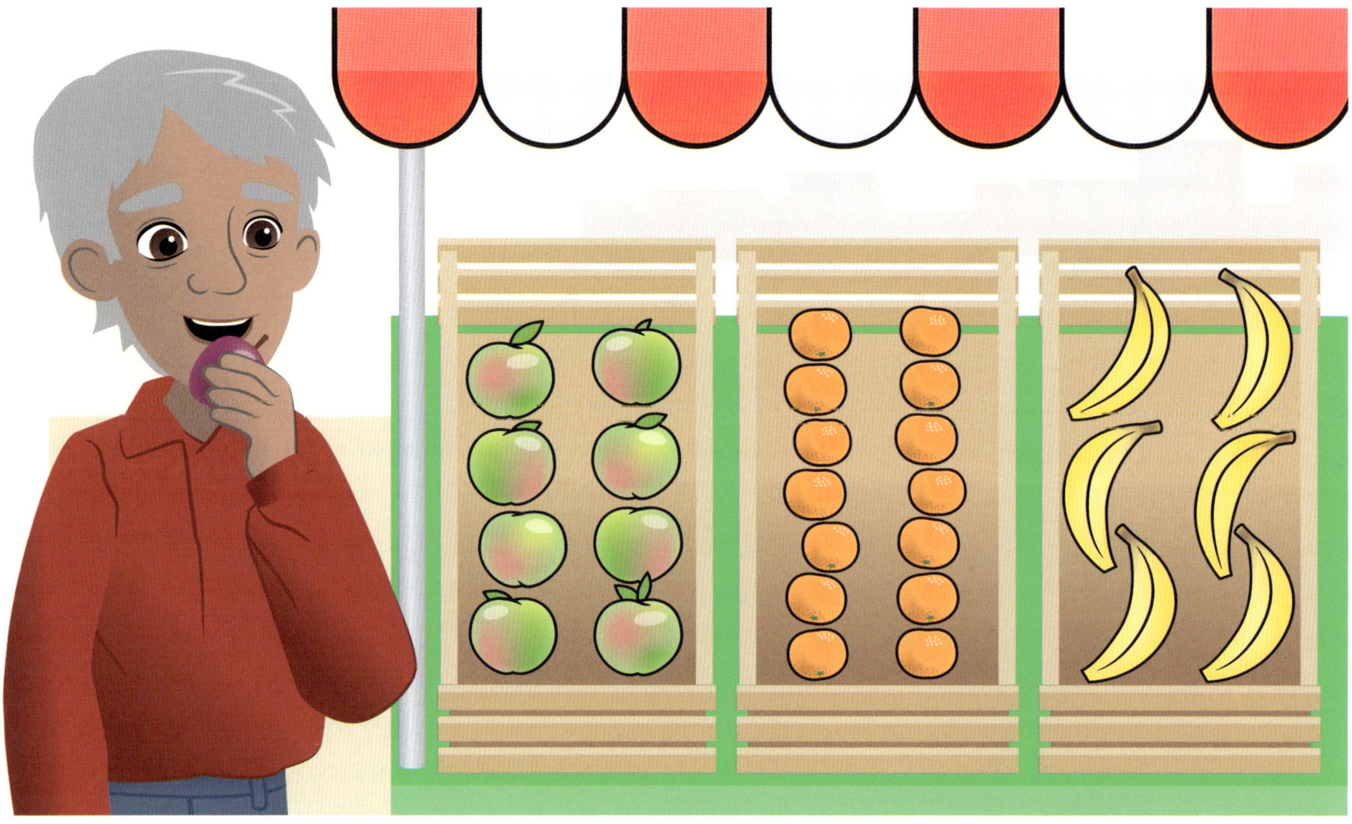

1 a) Draw a pictogram to represent the number of each type of fruit.

Use this key. | Each ● represents 2 pieces of fruit.

b) Why do you think it is better to use a ● to represent 2 pieces of fruit and not 1 piece?

Share

a)

Fruit	Pieces of fruit
apples	●●●●
oranges	●●●●●●●
bananas	●●●

Each ● represents 2 pieces of fruit.

b) When you use a ● to represent 2 pieces of fruit, you do not need to draw as many circles.

Oranges would look like this with one ● for 1 piece of fruit.

Oranges	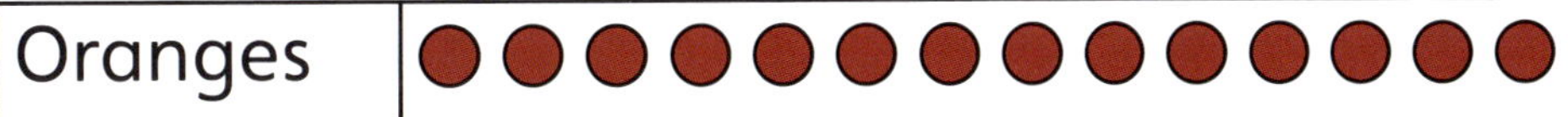

Think together

1 Reena counts the number of questions that 4 people answer correctly in a quiz. The tally chart shows her results.

Name	Tally	Number of questions
Leo	卌 卌 卌 卌	20
Jane	卌 卌 卌 卌 卌 卌 卌	35
Milo	卌 卌 卌	15
Amir	卌 卌 卌 卌 卌	25

Complete the pictogram for Reena's data.

Leo	⭐ ⭐ ⭐ ⭐
Jane	
Milo	
Amir	

Each ⭐ represents 5 questions.

2 Complete a pictogram to represent this data.

Favourite flavour	Number of children
Strawberry	40
Vanilla	60
Chocolate	70

Use 😊 to represent 10 children.

3 Josh counts the number of red sheets and blue sheets of paper.

Colour	Number of sheets
Blue	14
Red	11

Complete a pictogram to represent the data.

Use ○ to represent 2 sheets of paper.

179

Interpret pictograms (1 to 2, 5 or 10)

Discover

Day	Number of hot dinners
Monday	◎◎◎◎◎◎◎
Tuesday	◎◎◎◎◎
Wednesday	◎◎◎◎◎◎
Thursday	◎◎
Friday	

1 **a)** How many hot dinners were made on Tuesday?

b) 35 dinners are needed on Friday.

How many ◎ do you need to draw?

Share

a)

Tuesday has 5 ⬤ .

Each ⬤ equals 5 hot dinners.

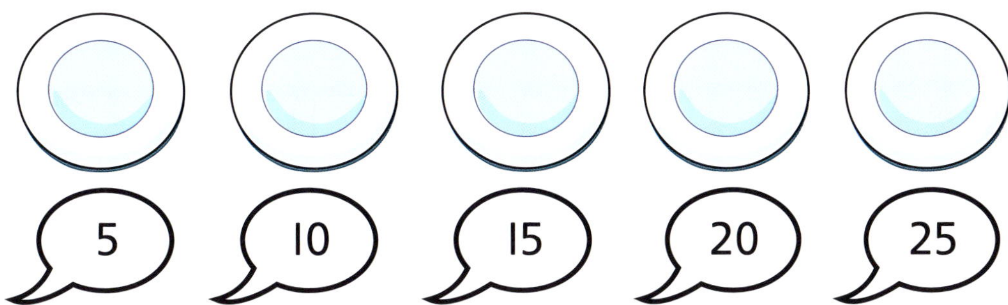

The key tells you how many each symbol represents

5 groups of 5 is equal to 25 hot dinners.

25 hot dinners were made on Tuesday.

b) 7 groups of 5 is equal to 35 hot dinners.

Each ⬤ represents 5 hot dinners.

I need to draw 7 ⬤ .

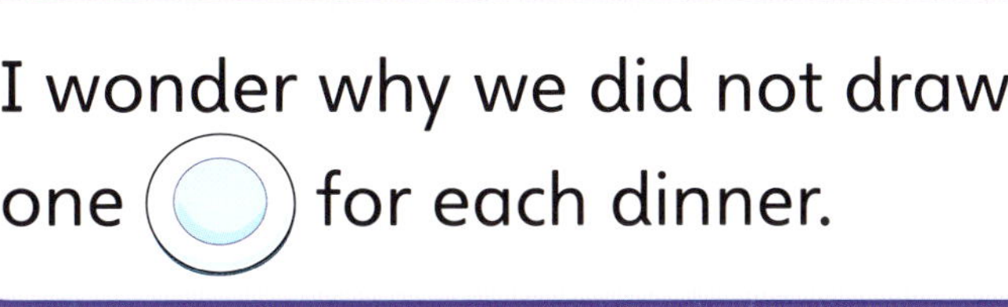

Think together

1 The pictogram shows the number of different types of birds in a garden.

Bird	Number of birds
blackbird	🐦 🐦 🐦
robin	🐦 🐦
sparrow	🐦
blue tit	🐦 🐦 🐦 🐦

a) How many of each bird were seen?

b) Which bird was seen the most?

c) How many fewer robins than blackbirds were seen?

2 Here is a pictogram.

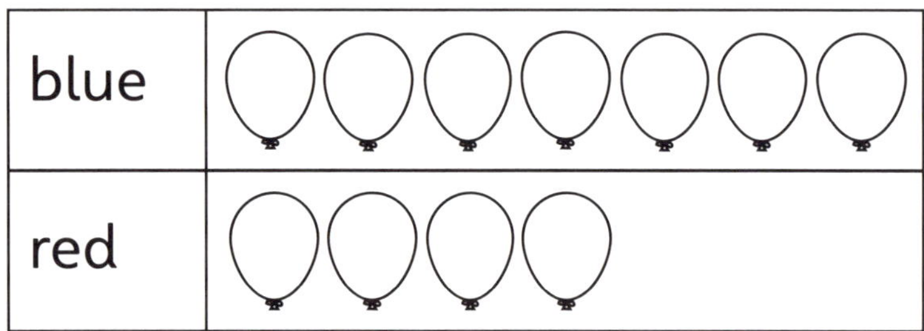

a) How many red balloons are there?

b) How many more blue balloons than red balloons are there?

3 This pictogram shows the number of books that the children read. Filip reads 10 books.

Child	Number of books
Filip	📙 📙 📙 📙 📙
Milo	📙 📙 📙
Bella	📙

Each 📙 represents 2 books.

Bella

Milo

Filip

Which statements are true?

→ **Practice book 2C p131**

End of unit check

1 Which tally chart shows the correct amount of flowers?

A

Flower	Tally
red	卌 ||
blue	|||
yellow	卌 ||
pink	卌 ||||
orange	卌 |||

C

Flower	Tally
red	卌	
blue	||||
yellow	卌 ||
pink	卌 卌
orange	卌 |||

B

Flower	Tally
red	卌	
blue	卌
yellow	卌 ||
pink	卌 |||
orange	卌 |||

D

Flower	Tally
red	卌
blue	||||
yellow	卌	
pink	卌 卌
orange	卌 |||

2 How many red apples are there?

- **A** $4\frac{1}{2}$
- **C** 5
- **B** 45
- **D** 50

green	🍏 🍏 🍏 🍏 🍏
red	🍎 🍎 🍎 🍎 🍎
pink	🍎 🍎 🍎

Each 🍎 represents 10 apples.

3 Which statement is true?

A There are 6 red tractors.

B There are 7 more blue tractors than yellow tractors.

C There are double the amount of orange tractors than yellow tractors.

D There are 8 blue tractors.

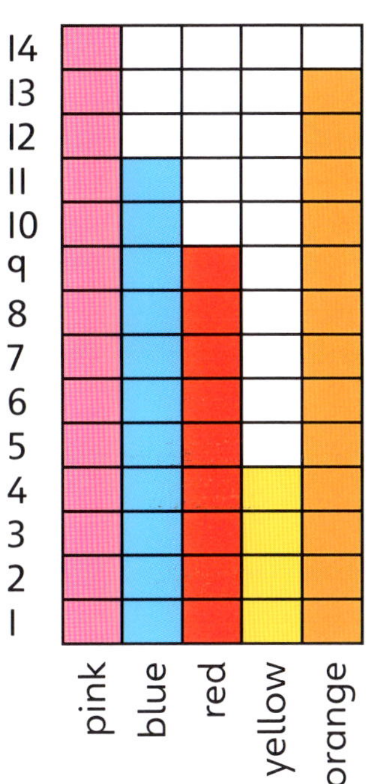

Think!

blue	
red	
yellow	
purple	

Each represents 5 cars.

Is Ola correct? Explain your answer.

Create your own sentences about this pictogram.

These words might help you.

equal · more than · less than

most · least · same as

difference · total

→ Practice book 2C p134

Practice helps us
get better!

I enjoyed finding new methods!

Wow, we have
solved some
difficult problems!

Yes, we have!
Can we find even
better ways to
solve problems?

It's always good to
learn new things.

What have we learnt?

- ⚡ Find a half and a quarter
- ⚡ Tell the time to 5 minutes
- ⚡ Solve addition and subtraction problems
- ⚡ Describe movement and turns
- ⚡ Draw and interpret charts and pictograms

Now you are ready for the next books!

Published by Pearson Education Limited, 80 Strand, London, WC2R 0RL.

www.pearsonschools.co.uk

Text © Pearson Education Limited 2017, 2023
Edited by Pearson and Florence Production Ltd
First edition edited by Pearson, Little Grey Cells Publishing Services and Haremi Ltd
Designed and typeset by Pearson and PDQ Digital Media Solutions Ltd
First edition designed and typeset by Kamae Design
Original illustrations © Pearson Education Limited 2017, 2023
Illustrated by Laura Arias, Fran and David Brylewski, Nigel Dobbyn and Nadene Naude at Beehive Illustration;
Emily Skinner at Graham-Cameron Illustration; Paul Higgins at Hunter-Higgins Illustrations; and Kamae Design
Images: The Royal Mint, 1971, 1982, 1990, 1992, 1997: 14, 85, 118; Bank of England: 100
Cover design by Pearson Education Ltd
Front and back cover illustrations by Will Overton at Advocate Art and Nadene Naude at Beehive Illustration

Series editor: Tony Staneff
Lead author: Josh Lury
Consultants (first edition): Professor Liu Jian and Professor Zhang Dan

The rights of Tony Staneff and Josh Lury to be identified as authors of this work have been asserted by them in accordance with the Copyright, Designs and Patents Act 1988.

First published 2017
This edition first published 2023

27 26 25
10 9 8 7 6 5

British Library Cataloguing in Publication Data
A catalogue record for this book is available from the British Library

ISBN 978 1 292 41950 3

Printed in the UK by Bell & Bain Ltd, Glasgow

For Power Maths resources go to
www.activelearnprimary.co.uk

Note from the publisher
Pearson has robust editorial processes, including answer and fact checks, to ensure the accuracy of the content in this publication, and every effort is made to ensure this publication is free of errors. We are, however, only human, and occasionally errors do occur. Pearson is not liable for any misunderstandings that arise as a result of errors in this publication, but it is our priority to ensure that the content is accurate. If you spot an error, please do contact us at resourcescorrections@pearson.com so we can make sure it is corrected.